C-4556   CAREER EXAMINATION SERIES

*This is your
PASSBOOK for...*

Traffic Court Clerk

*Test Preparation Study Guide
Questions & Answers*

COPYRIGHT NOTICE

This book is SOLELY intended for, is sold ONLY to, and its use is RESTRICTED to individual, bona fide applicants or candidates who qualify by virtue of having seriously filed applications for appropriate license, certificate, professional and/or promotional advancement, higher school matriculation, scholarship, or other legitimate requirements of education and/or governmental authorities.

This book is NOT intended for use, class instruction, tutoring, training, duplication, copying, reprinting, excerption, or adaptation, etc., by:

1) Other publishers
2) Proprietors and/or Instructors of "Coaching" and/or Preparatory Courses
3) Personnel and/or Training Divisions of commercial, industrial, and governmental organizations
4) Schools, colleges, or universities and/or their departments and staffs, including teachers and other personnel
5) Testing Agencies or Bureaus
6) Study groups which seek by the purchase of a single volume to copy and/or duplicate and/or adapt this material for use by the group as a whole without having purchased individual volumes for each of the members of the group
7) Et al.

Such persons would be in violation of appropriate Federal and State statutes.

PROVISION OF LICENSING AGREEMENTS – Recognized educational, commercial, industrial, and governmental institutions and organizations, and others legitimately engaged in educational pursuits, including training, testing, and measurement activities, may address request for a licensing agreement to the copyright owners, who will determine whether, and under what conditions, including fees and charges, the materials in this book may be used them. In other words, a licensing facility exists for the legitimate use of the material in this book on other than an individual basis. However, it is asseverated and affirmed here that the material in this book CANNOT be used without the receipt of the express permission of such a licensing agreement from the Publishers. Inquiries re licensing should be addressed to the company, attention rights and permissions department.

All rights reserved, including the right of reproduction in whole or in part, in any form or by any means, electronic or mechanical, including photocopying, recording, or by any information storage and retrieval system, without permission in writing from the Publisher.

Copyright © 2024 by
National Learning Corporation

212 Michael Drive, Syosset, NY 11791
(516) 921-8888 • www.passbooks.com
E-mail: info@passbooks.com

PUBLISHED IN THE UNITED STATES OF AMERICA

PASSBOOK® SERIES

THE *PASSBOOK® SERIES* has been created to prepare applicants and candidates for the ultimate academic battlefield – the examination room.

At some time in our lives, each and every one of us may be required to take an examination – for validation, matriculation, admission, qualification, registration, certification, or licensure.

Based on the assumption that every applicant or candidate has met the basic formal educational standards, has taken the required number of courses, and read the necessary texts, the *PASSBOOK® SERIES* furnishes the one special preparation which may assure passing with confidence, instead of failing with insecurity. Examination questions – together with answers – are furnished as the basic vehicle for study so that the mysteries of the examination and its compounding difficulties may be eliminated or diminished by a sure method.

This book is meant to help you pass your examination provided that you qualify and are serious in your objective.

The entire field is reviewed through the huge store of content information which is succinctly presented through a provocative and challenging approach – the question-and-answer method.

A climate of success is established by furnishing the correct answers at the end of each test.

You soon learn to recognize types of questions, forms of questions, and patterns of questioning. You may even begin to anticipate expected outcomes.

You perceive that many questions are repeated or adapted so that you can gain acute insights, which may enable you to score many sure points.

You learn how to confront new questions, or types of questions, and to attack them confidently and work out the correct answers.

You note objectives and emphases, and recognize pitfalls and dangers, so that you may make positive educational adjustments.

Moreover, you are kept fully informed in relation to new concepts, methods, practices, and directions in the field.

You discover that you are actually taking the examination all the time: you are preparing for the examination by "taking" an examination, not by reading extraneous and/or supererogatory textbooks.

In short, this PASSBOOK®, used directedly, should be an important factor in helping you to pass your test.

TRAFFIC COURT CLERK

DUTIES
An employee in this class performs varied clerical work relating to Traffic Court functions, requiring some knowledge of statutes and laws governing the practices and procedures of Traffic Courts. All work is performed according to standard procedures prescribed by state law, judicial determination and administrative directives. Work involves contact with attorneys and the general public regarding court functions and procedures. Work is performed under the supervision of a clerical or administrative supervisor. Does related work as required.

SCOPE OF THE EXAMINATION
The written test will cover knowledge, skills, and/or abilities in such areas as:
1. Understanding and interpreting written material;
2. Understanding and applying court rules and procedures;
3. Record keeping and organization of data including basic arithmetic computations;
4. Clerical operations including proofreading;
5. Traffic court terminology.

HOW TO TAKE A TEST

I. YOU MUST PASS AN EXAMINATION

A. WHAT EVERY CANDIDATE SHOULD KNOW

Examination applicants often ask us for help in preparing for the written test. What can I study in advance? What kinds of questions will be asked? How will the test be given? How will the papers be graded?

As an applicant for a civil service examination, you may be wondering about some of these things. Our purpose here is to suggest effective methods of advance study and to describe civil service examinations.

Your chances for success on this examination can be increased if you know how to prepare. Those "pre-examination jitters" can be reduced if you know what to expect. You can even experience an adventure in good citizenship if you know why civil service exams are given.

B. WHY ARE CIVIL SERVICE EXAMINATIONS GIVEN?

Civil service examinations are important to you in two ways. As a citizen, you want public jobs filled by employees who know how to do their work. As a job seeker, you want a fair chance to compete for that job on an equal footing with other candidates. The best-known means of accomplishing this two-fold goal is the competitive examination.

Exams are widely publicized throughout the nation. They may be administered for jobs in federal, state, city, municipal, town or village governments or agencies.

Any citizen may apply, with some limitations, such as the age or residence of applicants. Your experience and education may be reviewed to see whether you meet the requirements for the particular examination. When these requirements exist, they are reasonable and applied consistently to all applicants. Thus, a competitive examination may cause you some uneasiness now, but it is your privilege and safeguard.

C. HOW ARE CIVIL SERVICE EXAMS DEVELOPED?

Examinations are carefully written by trained technicians who are specialists in the field known as "psychological measurement," in consultation with recognized authorities in the field of work that the test will cover. These experts recommend the subject matter areas or skills to be tested; only those knowledges or skills important to your success on the job are included. The most reliable books and source materials available are used as references. Together, the experts and technicians judge the difficulty level of the questions.

Test technicians know how to phrase questions so that the problem is clearly stated. Their ethics do not permit "trick" or "catch" questions. Questions may have been tried out on sample groups, or subjected to statistical analysis, to determine their usefulness.

Written tests are often used in combination with performance tests, ratings of training and experience, and oral interviews. All of these measures combine to form the best-known means of finding the right person for the right job.

II. HOW TO PASS THE WRITTEN TEST

A. NATURE OF THE EXAMINATION

To prepare intelligently for civil service examinations, you should know how they differ from school examinations you have taken. In school you were assigned certain definite pages to read or subjects to cover. The examination questions were quite detailed and usually emphasized memory. Civil service exams, on the other hand, try to discover your present ability to perform the duties of a position, plus your potentiality to learn these duties. In other words, a civil service exam attempts to predict how successful you will be. Questions cover such a broad area that they cannot be as minute and detailed as school exam questions.

In the public service similar kinds of work, or positions, are grouped together in one "class." This process is known as *position-classification*. All the positions in a class are paid according to the salary range for that class. One class title covers all of these positions, and they are all tested by the same examination.

B. FOUR BASIC STEPS

1) Study the announcement

How, then, can you know what subjects to study? Our best answer is: "Learn as much as possible about the class of positions for which you've applied." The exam will test the knowledge, skills and abilities needed to do the work.

Your most valuable source of information about the position you want is the official exam announcement. This announcement lists the training and experience qualifications. Check these standards and apply only if you come reasonably close to meeting them.

The brief description of the position in the examination announcement offers some clues to the subjects which will be tested. Think about the job itself. Review the duties in your mind. Can you perform them, or are there some in which you are rusty? Fill in the blank spots in your preparation.

Many jurisdictions preview the written test in the exam announcement by including a section called "Knowledge and Abilities Required," "Scope of the Examination," or some similar heading. Here you will find out specifically what fields will be tested.

2) Review your own background

Once you learn in general what the position is all about, and what you need to know to do the work, ask yourself which subjects you already know fairly well and which need improvement. You may wonder whether to concentrate on improving your strong areas or on building some background in your fields of weakness. When the announcement has specified "some knowledge" or "considerable knowledge," or has used adjectives like "beginning principles of..." or "advanced ... methods," you can get a clue as to the number and difficulty of questions to be asked in any given field. More questions, and hence broader coverage, would be included for those subjects which are more important in the work. Now weigh your strengths and weaknesses against the job requirements and prepare accordingly.

3) Determine the level of the position

Another way to tell how intensively you should prepare is to understand the level of the job for which you are applying. Is it the entering level? In other words, is this the position in which beginners in a field of work are hired? Or is it an intermediate or advanced level? Sometimes this is indicated by such words as "Junior" or "Senior" in the class title. Other jurisdictions use Roman numerals to designate the level – Clerk I, Clerk II, for example. The word "Supervisor" sometimes appears in the title. If the level is not indicated by the title, check the description of duties. Will you be working under very close supervision, or will you have responsibility for independent decisions in this work?

4) Choose appropriate study materials

Now that you know the subjects to be examined and the relative amount of each subject to be covered, you can choose suitable study materials. For beginning level jobs, or even advanced ones, if you have a pronounced weakness in some aspect of your training, read a modern, standard textbook in that field. Be sure it is up to date and has general coverage. Such books are normally available at your library, and the librarian will be glad to help you locate one. For entry-level positions, questions of appropriate difficulty are chosen – neither highly advanced questions, nor those too simple. Such questions require careful thought but not advanced training.

If the position for which you are applying is technical or advanced, you will read more advanced, specialized material. If you are already familiar with the basic principles of your field, elementary textbooks would waste your time. Concentrate on advanced textbooks and technical periodicals. Think through the concepts and review difficult problems in your field.

These are all general sources. You can get more ideas on your own initiative, following these leads. For example, training manuals and publications of the government agency which employs workers in your field can be useful, particularly for technical and professional positions. A letter or visit to the government department involved may result in more specific study suggestions, and certainly will provide you with a more definite idea of the exact nature of the position you are seeking.

III. KINDS OF TESTS

Tests are used for purposes other than measuring knowledge and ability to perform specified duties. For some positions, it is equally important to test ability to make adjustments to new situations or to profit from training. In others, basic mental abilities not dependent on information are essential. Questions which test these things may not appear as pertinent to the duties of the position as those which test for knowledge and information. Yet they are often highly important parts of a fair examination. For very general questions, it is almost impossible to help you direct your study efforts. What we can do is to point out some of the more common of these general abilities needed in public service positions and describe some typical questions.

1) General information

Broad, general information has been found useful for predicting job success in some kinds of work. This is tested in a variety of ways, from vocabulary lists to questions about current events. Basic background in some field of work, such as sociology or economics, may be sampled in a group of questions. Often these are principles which have become familiar to most persons through exposure rather than through formal training. It is difficult to advise you how to study for these questions; being alert to the world around you is our best suggestion.

2) Verbal ability

An example of an ability needed in many positions is verbal or language ability. Verbal ability is, in brief, the ability to use and understand words. Vocabulary and grammar tests are typical measures of this ability. Reading comprehension or paragraph interpretation questions are common in many kinds of civil service tests. You are given a paragraph of written material and asked to find its central meaning.

3) Numerical ability

Number skills can be tested by the familiar arithmetic problem, by checking paired lists of numbers to see which are alike and which are different, or by interpreting charts and graphs. In the latter test, a graph may be printed in the test booklet which you are asked to use as the basis for answering questions.

4) Observation

A popular test for law-enforcement positions is the observation test. A picture is shown to you for several minutes, then taken away. Questions about the picture test your ability to observe both details and larger elements.

5) Following directions

In many positions in the public service, the employee must be able to carry out written instructions dependably and accurately. You may be given a chart with several columns, each column listing a variety of information. The questions require you to carry out directions involving the information given in the chart.

6) Skills and aptitudes

Performance tests effectively measure some manual skills and aptitudes. When the skill is one in which you are trained, such as typing or shorthand, you can practice. These tests are often very much like those given in business school or high school courses. For many of the other skills and aptitudes, however, no short-time preparation can be made. Skills and abilities natural to you or that you have developed throughout your lifetime are being tested.

Many of the general questions just described provide all the data needed to answer the questions and ask you to use your reasoning ability to find the answers. Your best preparation for these tests, as well as for tests of facts and ideas, is to be at your physical and mental best. You, no doubt, have your own methods of getting into an exam-taking mood and keeping "in shape." The next section lists some ideas on this subject.

IV. KINDS OF QUESTIONS

Only rarely is the "essay" question, which you answer in narrative form, used in civil service tests. Civil service tests are usually of the short-answer type. Full instructions for answering these questions will be given to you at the examination. But in case this is your first experience with short-answer questions and separate answer sheets, here is what you need to know:

1) Multiple-choice Questions

Most popular of the short-answer questions is the "multiple choice" or "best answer" question. It can be used, for example, to test for factual knowledge, ability to solve problems or judgment in meeting situations found at work.

A multiple-choice question is normally one of three types—
- It can begin with an incomplete statement followed by several possible endings. You are to find the one ending which *best* completes the statement, although some of the others may not be entirely wrong.
- It can also be a complete statement in the form of a question which is answered by choosing one of the statements listed.

- It can be in the form of a problem – again you select the best answer.

Here is an example of a multiple-choice question with a discussion which should give you some clues as to the method for choosing the right answer:

When an employee has a complaint about his assignment, the action which will *best* help him overcome his difficulty is to
- A. discuss his difficulty with his coworkers
- B. take the problem to the head of the organization
- C. take the problem to the person who gave him the assignment
- D. say nothing to anyone about his complaint

In answering this question, you should study each of the choices to find which is best. Consider choice "A" – Certainly an employee may discuss his complaint with fellow employees, but no change or improvement can result, and the complaint remains unresolved. Choice "B" is a poor choice since the head of the organization probably does not know what assignment you have been given, and taking your problem to him is known as "going over the head" of the supervisor. The supervisor, or person who made the assignment, is the person who can clarify it or correct any injustice. Choice "C" is, therefore, correct. To say nothing, as in choice "D," is unwise. Supervisors have and interest in knowing the problems employees are facing, and the employee is seeking a solution to his problem.

2) True/False Questions

The "true/false" or "right/wrong" form of question is sometimes used. Here a complete statement is given. Your job is to decide whether the statement is right or wrong.

SAMPLE: A roaming cell-phone call to a nearby city costs less than a non-roaming call to a distant city.

This statement is wrong, or false, since roaming calls are more expensive.

This is not a complete list of all possible question forms, although most of the others are variations of these common types. You will always get complete directions for answering questions. Be sure you understand *how* to mark your answers – ask questions until you do.

V. RECORDING YOUR ANSWERS

Computer terminals are used more and more today for many different kinds of exams.

For an examination with very few applicants, you may be told to record your answers in the test booklet itself. Separate answer sheets are much more common. If this separate answer sheet is to be scored by machine – and this is often the case – it is highly important that you mark your answers correctly in order to get credit.

An electronic scoring machine is often used in civil service offices because of the speed with which papers can be scored. Machine-scored answer sheets must be marked with a pencil, which will be given to you. This pencil has a high graphite content which responds to the electronic scoring machine. As a matter of fact, stray dots may register as answers, so do not let your pencil rest on the answer sheet while you are pondering the correct answer. Also, if your pencil lead breaks or is otherwise defective, ask for another.

Since the answer sheet will be dropped in a slot in the scoring machine, be careful not to bend the corners or get the paper crumpled.

The answer sheet normally has five vertical columns of numbers, with 30 numbers to a column. These numbers correspond to the question numbers in your test booklet. After each number, going across the page are four or five pairs of dotted lines. These short dotted lines have small letters or numbers above them. The first two pairs may also have a "T" or "F" above the letters. This indicates that the first two pairs only are to be used if the questions are of the true-false type. If the questions are multiple choice, disregard the "T" and "F" and pay attention only to the small letters or numbers.

Answer your questions in the manner of the sample that follows:

32. The largest city in the United States is
    A. Washington, D.C.
    B. New York City
    C. Chicago
    D. Detroit
    E. San Francisco

1) Choose the answer you think is best. (New York City is the largest, so "B" is correct.)
2) Find the row of dotted lines numbered the same as the question you are answering. (Find row number 32)
3) Find the pair of dotted lines corresponding to the answer. (Find the pair of lines under the mark "B.")
4) Make a solid black mark between the dotted lines.

VI. BEFORE THE TEST

Common sense will help you find procedures to follow to get ready for an examination. Too many of us, however, overlook these sensible measures. Indeed, nervousness and fatigue have been found to be the most serious reasons why applicants fail to do their best on civil service tests. Here is a list of reminders:

- Begin your preparation early – Don't wait until the last minute to go scurrying around for books and materials or to find out what the position is all about.
- Prepare continuously – An hour a night for a week is better than an all-night cram session. This has been definitely established. What is more, a night a week for a month will return better dividends than crowding your study into a shorter period of time.
- Locate the place of the exam – You have been sent a notice telling you when and where to report for the examination. If the location is in a different town or otherwise unfamiliar to you, it would be well to inquire the best route and learn something about the building.
- Relax the night before the test – Allow your mind to rest. Do not study at all that night. Plan some mild recreation or diversion; then go to bed early and get a good night's sleep.
- Get up early enough to make a leisurely trip to the place for the test – This way unforeseen events, traffic snarls, unfamiliar buildings, etc. will not upset you.
- Dress comfortably – A written test is not a fashion show. You will be known by number and not by name, so wear something comfortable.

- Leave excess paraphernalia at home – Shopping bags and odd bundles will get in your way. You need bring only the items mentioned in the official notice you received; usually everything you need is provided. Do not bring reference books to the exam. They will only confuse those last minutes and be taken away from you when in the test room.
- Arrive somewhat ahead of time – If because of transportation schedules you must get there very early, bring a newspaper or magazine to take your mind off yourself while waiting.
- Locate the examination room – When you have found the proper room, you will be directed to the seat or part of the room where you will sit. Sometimes you are given a sheet of instructions to read while you are waiting. Do not fill out any forms until you are told to do so; just read them and be prepared.
- Relax and prepare to listen to the instructions
- If you have any physical problem that may keep you from doing your best, be sure to tell the test administrator. If you are sick or in poor health, you really cannot do your best on the exam. You can come back and take the test some other time.

VII. AT THE TEST

The day of the test is here and you have the test booklet in your hand. The temptation to get going is very strong. Caution! There is more to success than knowing the right answers. You must know how to identify your papers and understand variations in the type of short-answer question used in this particular examination. Follow these suggestions for maximum results from your efforts:

1) Cooperate with the monitor

The test administrator has a duty to create a situation in which you can be as much at ease as possible. He will give instructions, tell you when to begin, check to see that you are marking your answer sheet correctly, and so on. He is not there to guard you, although he will see that your competitors do not take unfair advantage. He wants to help you do your best.

2) Listen to all instructions

Don't jump the gun! Wait until you understand all directions. In most civil service tests you get more time than you need to answer the questions. So don't be in a hurry. Read each word of instructions until you clearly understand the meaning. Study the examples, listen to all announcements and follow directions. Ask questions if you do not understand what to do.

3) Identify your papers

Civil service exams are usually identified by number only. You will be assigned a number; you must not put your name on your test papers. Be sure to copy your number correctly. Since more than one exam may be given, copy your exact examination title.

4) Plan your time

Unless you are told that a test is a "speed" or "rate of work" test, speed itself is usually not important. Time enough to answer all the questions will be provided, but this does not mean that you have all day. An overall time limit has been set. Divide the total time (in minutes) by the number of questions to determine the approximate time you have for each question.

5) Do not linger over difficult questions

If you come across a difficult question, mark it with a paper clip (useful to have along) and come back to it when you have been through the booklet. One caution if you do this – be sure to skip a number on your answer sheet as well. Check often to be sure that you have not lost your place and that you are marking in the row numbered the same as the question you are answering.

6) Read the questions

Be sure you know what the question asks! Many capable people are unsuccessful because they failed to *read* the questions correctly.

7) Answer all questions

Unless you have been instructed that a penalty will be deducted for incorrect answers, it is better to guess than to omit a question.

8) Speed tests

It is often better NOT to guess on speed tests. It has been found that on timed tests people are tempted to spend the last few seconds before time is called in marking answers at random – without even reading them – in the hope of picking up a few extra points. To discourage this practice, the instructions may warn you that your score will be "corrected" for guessing. That is, a penalty will be applied. The incorrect answers will be deducted from the correct ones, or some other penalty formula will be used.

9) Review your answers

If you finish before time is called, go back to the questions you guessed or omitted to give them further thought. Review other answers if you have time.

10) Return your test materials

If you are ready to leave before others have finished or time is called, take ALL your materials to the monitor and leave quietly. Never take any test material with you. The monitor can discover whose papers are not complete, and taking a test booklet may be grounds for disqualification.

VIII. EXAMINATION TECHNIQUES

1) Read the general instructions carefully. These are usually printed on the first page of the exam booklet. As a rule, these instructions refer to the timing of the examination; the fact that you should not start work until the signal and must stop work at a signal, etc. If there are any *special* instructions, such as a choice of questions to be answered, make sure that you note this instruction carefully.

2) When you are ready to start work on the examination, that is as soon as the signal has been given, read the instructions to each question booklet, underline any key words or phrases, such as *least, best, outline, describe* and the like. In this way you will tend to answer as requested rather than discover on reviewing your paper that you *listed without describing*, that you selected the *worst* choice rather than the *best* choice, etc.

3) If the examination is of the objective or multiple-choice type – that is, each question will also give a series of possible answers: A, B, C or D, and you are called upon to select the best answer and write the letter next to that answer on your answer paper – it is advisable to start answering each question in turn. There may be anywhere from 50 to 100 such questions in the three or four hours allotted and you can see how much time would be taken if you read through all the questions before beginning to answer any. Furthermore, if you come across a question or group of questions which you know would be difficult to answer, it would undoubtedly affect your handling of all the other questions.

4) If the examination is of the essay type and contains but a few questions, it is a moot point as to whether you should read all the questions before starting to answer any one. Of course, if you are given a choice – say five out of seven and the like – then it is essential to read all the questions so you can eliminate the two that are most difficult. If, however, you are asked to answer all the questions, there may be danger in trying to answer the easiest one first because you may find that you will spend too much time on it. The best technique is to answer the first question, then proceed to the second, etc.

5) Time your answers. Before the exam begins, write down the time it started, then add the time allowed for the examination and write down the time it must be completed, then divide the time available somewhat as follows:
    - If 3-1/2 hours are allowed, that would be 210 minutes. If you have 80 objective-type questions, that would be an average of 2-1/2 minutes per question. Allow yourself no more than 2 minutes per question, or a total of 160 minutes, which will permit about 50 minutes to review.
    - If for the time allotment of 210 minutes there are 7 essay questions to answer, that would average about 30 minutes a question. Give yourself only 25 minutes per question so that you have about 35 minutes to review.

6) The most important instruction is to *read each question* and make sure you know what is wanted. The second most important instruction is to *time yourself properly* so that you answer every question. The third most important instruction is to *answer every question*. Guess if you have to but include something for each question. Remember that you will receive no credit for a blank and will probably receive some credit if you write something in answer to an essay question. If you guess a letter – say "B" for a multiple-choice question – you may have guessed right. If you leave a blank as an answer to a multiple-choice question, the examiners may respect your feelings but it will not add a point to your score. Some exams may penalize you for wrong answers, so in such cases *only*, you may not want to guess unless you have some basis for your answer.

7) Suggestions
    a. Objective-type questions
        1. Examine the question booklet for proper sequence of pages and questions
        2. Read all instructions carefully
        3. Skip any question which seems too difficult; return to it after all other questions have been answered
        4. Apportion your time properly; do not spend too much time on any single question or group of questions

5. Note and underline key words – *all, most, fewest, least, best, worst, same, opposite,* etc.
6. Pay particular attention to negatives
7. Note unusual option, e.g., unduly long, short, complex, different or similar in content to the body of the question
8. Observe the use of "hedging" words – *probably, may, most likely,* etc.
9. Make sure that your answer is put next to the same number as the question
10. Do not second-guess unless you have good reason to believe the second answer is definitely more correct
11. Cross out original answer if you decide another answer is more accurate; do not erase until you are ready to hand your paper in
12. Answer all questions; guess unless instructed otherwise
13. Leave time for review

   b. Essay questions
     1. Read each question carefully
     2. Determine exactly what is wanted. Underline key words or phrases.
     3. Decide on outline or paragraph answer
     4. Include many different points and elements unless asked to develop any one or two points or elements
     5. Show impartiality by giving pros and cons unless directed to select one side only
     6. Make and write down any assumptions you find necessary to answer the questions
     7. Watch your English, grammar, punctuation and choice of words
     8. Time your answers; don't crowd material

8) Answering the essay question

Most essay questions can be answered by framing the specific response around several key words or ideas. Here are a few such key words or ideas:

M's: manpower, materials, methods, money, management
P's: purpose, program, policy, plan, procedure, practice, problems, pitfalls, personnel, public relations

   a. Six basic steps in handling problems:
     1. Preliminary plan and background development
     2. Collect information, data and facts
     3. Analyze and interpret information, data and facts
     4. Analyze and develop solutions as well as make recommendations
     5. Prepare report and sell recommendations
     6. Install recommendations and follow up effectiveness

   b. Pitfalls to avoid
     1. *Taking things for granted* – A statement of the situation does not necessarily imply that each of the elements is necessarily true; for example, a complaint may be invalid and biased so that all that can be taken for granted is that a complaint has been registered

2. *Considering only one side of a situation* – Wherever possible, indicate several alternatives and then point out the reasons you selected the best one
3. *Failing to indicate follow up* – Whenever your answer indicates action on your part, make certain that you will take proper follow-up action to see how successful your recommendations, procedures or actions turn out to be
4. *Taking too long in answering any single question* – Remember to time your answers properly

IX. AFTER THE TEST

Scoring procedures differ in detail among civil service jurisdictions although the general principles are the same. Whether the papers are hand-scored or graded by machine we have described, they are nearly always graded by number. That is, the person who marks the paper knows only the number – never the name – of the applicant. Not until all the papers have been graded will they be matched with names. If other tests, such as training and experience or oral interview ratings have been given, scores will be combined. Different parts of the examination usually have different weights. For example, the written test might count 60 percent of the final grade, and a rating of training and experience 40 percent. In many jurisdictions, veterans will have a certain number of points added to their grades.

After the final grade has been determined, the names are placed in grade order and an eligible list is established. There are various methods for resolving ties between those who get the same final grade – probably the most common is to place first the name of the person whose application was received first. Job offers are made from the eligible list in the order the names appear on it. You will be notified of your grade and your rank as soon as all these computations have been made. This will be done as rapidly as possible.

People who are found to meet the requirements in the announcement are called "eligibles." Their names are put on a list of eligible candidates. An eligible's chances of getting a job depend on how high he stands on this list and how fast agencies are filling jobs from the list.

When a job is to be filled from a list of eligibles, the agency asks for the names of people on the list of eligibles for that job. When the civil service commission receives this request, it sends to the agency the names of the three people highest on this list. Or, if the job to be filled has specialized requirements, the office sends the agency the names of the top three persons who meet these requirements from the general list.

The appointing officer makes a choice from among the three people whose names were sent to him. If the selected person accepts the appointment, the names of the others are put back on the list to be considered for future openings.

That is the rule in hiring from all kinds of eligible lists, whether they are for typist, carpenter, chemist, or something else. For every vacancy, the appointing officer has his choice of any one of the top three eligibles on the list. This explains why the person whose name is on top of the list sometimes does not get an appointment when some of the persons lower on the list do. If the appointing officer chooses the second or third eligible, the No. 1 eligible does not get a job at once, but stays on the list until he is appointed or the list is terminated.

X. HOW TO PASS THE INTERVIEW TEST

The examination for which you applied requires an oral interview test. You have already taken the written test and you are now being called for the interview test – the final part of the formal examination.

You may think that it is not possible to prepare for an interview test and that there are no procedures to follow during an interview. Our purpose is to point out some things you can do in advance that will help you and some good rules to follow and pitfalls to avoid while you are being interviewed.

What is an interview supposed to test?

The written examination is designed to test the technical knowledge and competence of the candidate; the oral is designed to evaluate intangible qualities, not readily measured otherwise, and to establish a list showing the relative fitness of each candidate – as measured against his competitors – for the position sought. Scoring is not on the basis of "right" and "wrong," but on a sliding scale of values ranging from "not passable" to "outstanding." As a matter of fact, it is possible to achieve a relatively low score without a single "incorrect" answer because of evident weakness in the qualities being measured.

Occasionally, an examination may consist entirely of an oral test – either an individual or a group oral. In such cases, information is sought concerning the technical knowledges and abilities of the candidate, since there has been no written examination for this purpose. More commonly, however, an oral test is used to supplement a written examination.

Who conducts interviews?

The composition of oral boards varies among different jurisdictions. In nearly all, a representative of the personnel department serves as chairman. One of the members of the board may be a representative of the department in which the candidate would work. In some cases, "outside experts" are used, and, frequently, a businessman or some other representative of the general public is asked to serve. Labor and management or other special groups may be represented. The aim is to secure the services of experts in the appropriate field.

However the board is composed, it is a good idea (and not at all improper or unethical) to ascertain in advance of the interview who the members are and what groups they represent. When you are introduced to them, you will have some idea of their backgrounds and interests, and at least you will not stutter and stammer over their names.

What should be done before the interview?

While knowledge about the board members is useful and takes some of the surprise element out of the interview, there is other preparation which is more substantive. It *is* possible to prepare for an oral interview – in several ways:

1) Keep a copy of your application and review it carefully before the interview

This may be the only document before the oral board, and the starting point of the interview. Know what education and experience you have listed there, and the sequence and dates of all of it. Sometimes the board will ask you to review the highlights of your experience for them; you should not have to hem and haw doing it.

2) Study the class specification and the examination announcement

Usually, the oral board has one or both of these to guide them. The qualities, characteristics or knowledges required by the position sought are stated in these documents. They offer valuable clues as to the nature of the oral interview. For example, if the job involves supervisory responsibilities, the announcement will usually indicate that knowledge of modern supervisory methods and the qualifications of the candidate as a supervisor will be tested. If so, you can expect such questions, frequently in the form of a hypothetical situation which you are expected to solve. NEVER go into an oral without knowledge of the duties and responsibilities of the job you seek.

3) Think through each qualification required

Try to visualize the kind of questions you would ask if you were a board member. How well could you answer them? Try especially to appraise your own knowledge and background in each area, *measured against the job sought*, and identify any areas in which you are weak. Be critical and realistic – do not flatter yourself.

4) Do some general reading in areas in which you feel you may be weak

For example, if the job involves supervision and your past experience has NOT, some general reading in supervisory methods and practices, particularly in the field of human relations, might be useful. Do NOT study agency procedures or detailed manuals. The oral board will be testing your understanding and capacity, not your memory.

5) Get a good night's sleep and watch your general health and mental attitude

You will want a clear head at the interview. Take care of a cold or any other minor ailment, and of course, no hangovers.

What should be done on the day of the interview?

Now comes the day of the interview itself. Give yourself plenty of time to get there. Plan to arrive somewhat ahead of the scheduled time, particularly if your appointment is in the fore part of the day. If a previous candidate fails to appear, the board might be ready for you a bit early. By early afternoon an oral board is almost invariably behind schedule if there are many candidates, and you may have to wait. Take along a book or magazine to read, or your application to review, but leave any extraneous material in the waiting room when you go in for your interview. In any event, relax and compose yourself.

The matter of dress is important. The board is forming impressions about you – from your experience, your manners, your attitude, and your appearance. Give your personal appearance careful attention. Dress your best, but not your flashiest. Choose conservative, appropriate clothing, and be sure it is immaculate. This is a business interview, and your appearance should indicate that you regard it as such. Besides, being well groomed and properly dressed will help boost your confidence.

Sooner or later, someone will call your name and escort you into the interview room. *This is it.* From here on you are on your own. It is too late for any more preparation. But remember, you asked for this opportunity to prove your fitness, and you are here because your request was granted.

What happens when you go in?

The usual sequence of events will be as follows: The clerk (who is often the board stenographer) will introduce you to the chairman of the oral board, who will introduce you to the other members of the board. Acknowledge the introductions before you sit down. Do not be surprised if you find a microphone facing you or a stenotypist sitting by. Oral interviews are usually recorded in the event of an appeal or other review.

Usually the chairman of the board will open the interview by reviewing the highlights of your education and work experience from your application – primarily for the benefit of the other members of the board, as well as to get the material into the record. Do not interrupt or comment unless there is an error or significant misinterpretation; if that is the case, do not hesitate. But do not quibble about insignificant matters. Also, he will usually ask you some question about your education, experience or your present job – partly to get you to start talking and to establish the interviewing "rapport." He may start the actual questioning, or turn it over to one of the other members. Frequently, each member undertakes the questioning on a particular area, one in which he is perhaps most competent, so you can expect each member to participate in the examination. Because time is limited, you may also expect some rather abrupt switches in the direction the questioning takes, so do not be upset by it. Normally, a board member will not pursue a single line of questioning unless he discovers a particular strength or weakness.

After each member has participated, the chairman will usually ask whether any member has any further questions, then will ask you if you have anything you wish to add. Unless you are expecting this question, it may floor you. Worse, it may start you off on an extended, extemporaneous speech. The board is not usually seeking more information. The question is principally to offer you a last opportunity to present further qualifications or to indicate that you have nothing to add. So, if you feel that a significant qualification or characteristic has been overlooked, it is proper to point it out in a sentence or so. Do not compliment the board on the thoroughness of their examination – they have been sketchy, and you know it. If you wish, merely say, "No thank you, I have nothing further to add." This is a point where you can "talk yourself out" of a good impression or fail to present an important bit of information. Remember, *you close the interview yourself*.

The chairman will then say, "That is all, Mr. _____, thank you." Do not be startled; the interview is over, and quicker than you think. Thank him, gather your belongings and take your leave. Save your sigh of relief for the other side of the door.

How to put your best foot forward

Throughout this entire process, you may feel that the board individually and collectively is trying to pierce your defenses, seek out your hidden weaknesses and embarrass and confuse you. Actually, this is not true. They are obliged to make an appraisal of your qualifications for the job you are seeking, and they want to see you in your best light. Remember, they must interview all candidates and a non-cooperative candidate may become a failure in spite of their best efforts to bring out his qualifications. Here are 15 suggestions that will help you:

1) Be natural – Keep your attitude confident, not cocky

If you are not confident that you can do the job, do not expect the board to be. Do not apologize for your weaknesses, try to bring out your strong points. The board is interested in a positive, not negative, presentation. Cockiness will antagonize any board member and make him wonder if you are covering up a weakness by a false show of strength.

2) Get comfortable, but don't lounge or sprawl

Sit erectly but not stiffly. A careless posture may lead the board to conclude that you are careless in other things, or at least that you are not impressed by the importance of the occasion. Either conclusion is natural, even if incorrect. Do not fuss with your clothing, a pencil or an ashtray. Your hands may occasionally be useful to emphasize a point; do not let them become a point of distraction.

3) Do not wisecrack or make small talk

This is a serious situation, and your attitude should show that you consider it as such. Further, the time of the board is limited – they do not want to waste it, and neither should you.

4) Do not exaggerate your experience or abilities

In the first place, from information in the application or other interviews and sources, the board may know more about you than you think. Secondly, you probably will not get away with it. An experienced board is rather adept at spotting such a situation, so do not take the chance.

5) If you know a board member, do not make a point of it, yet do not hide it

Certainly you are not fooling him, and probably not the other members of the board. Do not try to take advantage of your acquaintanceship – it will probably do you little good.

6) Do not dominate the interview

Let the board do that. They will give you the clues – do not assume that you have to do all the talking. Realize that the board has a number of questions to ask you, and do not try to take up all the interview time by showing off your extensive knowledge of the answer to the first one.

7) Be attentive

You only have 20 minutes or so, and you should keep your attention at its sharpest throughout. When a member is addressing a problem or question to you, give him your undivided attention. Address your reply principally to him, but do not exclude the other board members.

8) Do not interrupt

A board member may be stating a problem for you to analyze. He will ask you a question when the time comes. Let him state the problem, and wait for the question.

9) Make sure you understand the question

Do not try to answer until you are sure what the question is. If it is not clear, restate it in your own words or ask the board member to clarify it for you. However, do not haggle about minor elements.

10) Reply promptly but not hastily

A common entry on oral board rating sheets is "candidate responded readily," or "candidate hesitated in replies." Respond as promptly and quickly as you can, but do not jump to a hasty, ill-considered answer.

11) Do not be peremptory in your answers

A brief answer is proper – but do not fire your answer back. That is a losing game from your point of view. The board member can probably ask questions much faster than you can answer them.

12) Do not try to create the answer you think the board member wants

He is interested in what kind of mind you have and how it works – not in playing games. Furthermore, he can usually spot this practice and will actually grade you down on it.

13) Do not switch sides in your reply merely to agree with a board member

Frequently, a member will take a contrary position merely to draw you out and to see if you are willing and able to defend your point of view. Do not start a debate, yet do not surrender a good position. If a position is worth taking, it is worth defending.

14) Do not be afraid to admit an error in judgment if you are shown to be wrong

The board knows that you are forced to reply without any opportunity for careful consideration. Your answer may be demonstrably wrong. If so, admit it and get on with the interview.

15) Do not dwell at length on your present job

The opening question may relate to your present assignment. Answer the question but do not go into an extended discussion. You are being examined for a *new* job, not your present one. As a matter of fact, try to phrase ALL your answers in terms of the job for which you are being examined.

Basis of Rating

Probably you will forget most of these "do's" and "don'ts" when you walk into the oral interview room. Even remembering them all will not ensure you a passing grade. Perhaps you did not have the qualifications in the first place. But remembering them will help you to put your best foot forward, without treading on the toes of the board members.

Rumor and popular opinion to the contrary notwithstanding, an oral board wants you to make the best appearance possible. They know you are under pressure – but they also want to see how you respond to it as a guide to what your reaction would be under the pressures of the job you seek. They will be influenced by the degree of poise you display, the personal traits you show and the manner in which you respond.

ABOUT THIS BOOK

This book contains tests divided into Examination Sections. Go through each test, answering every question in the margin. We have also attached a sample answer sheet at the back of the book that can be removed and used. At the end of each test look at the answer key and check your answers. On the ones you got wrong, look at the right answer choice and learn. Do not fill in the answers first. Do not memorize the questions and answers, but understand the answer and principles involved. On your test, the questions will likely be different from the samples. Questions are changed and new ones added. If you understand these past questions you should have success with any changes that arise. Tests may consist of several types of questions. We have additional books on each subject should more study be advisable or necessary for you. Finally, the more you study, the better prepared you will be. This book is intended to be the last thing you study before you walk into the examination room. Prior study of relevant texts is also recommended. NLC publishes some of these in our Fundamental Series. Knowledge and good sense are important factors in passing your exam. Good luck also helps. So now study this Passbook, absorb the material contained within and take that knowledge into the examination. Then do your best to pass that exam.

EXAMINATION SECTION

EXAMINATION SECTION
TEST 1

DIRECTIONS: Each question or incomplete statement is followed by several suggested answers or completions. Select the one that BEST answers the question or completes the statement. *PRINT THE LETTER OF THE CORRECT ANSWER IN THE SPACE AT THE RIGHT.*

Questions 1-6.

DIRECTIONS: Questions 1 through 6 consist of descriptions of material to which a filing designation must be assigned.

Assume that the matters and cases described in the questions were referred for handling to a government legal office which has its files set up according to these file designations. The file designation consists of a number of characters and punctuation marks as described below.

The first character refers to agencies whose legal work is handled by this office. These agencies are numbered consecutively in the order in which they first submit a matter for attention, and are identified in an alphabetical card index. To date numbers have been assigned to agencies as follows:

Department of Correction	1
Police Department	2
Department of Traffic	3
Department of Consumer Affairs	4
Commission on Human Rights	5
Board of Elections	6
Department of Personnel	7
Board of Estimate	8

The second character is separated from the first character by a dash. The second character is the last digit of the year in which a particular lawsuit or matter is referred to the legal office.

The third character is separated from the second character by a colon and may consist of either of the following:

I. A sub-number assigned to each lawsuit to which the agency is a party. Lawsuits are numbered consecutively regardless of year. (Lawsuits are brought by or against agency heads rather than agencies themselves, but references are made to agencies for the purpose of simplification.)

or II. A capital letter assigned to each matter other than a lawsuit according to subject, the subject being identified in an alphabetical index. To date, letters have been assigned to subjects as follows:

Citizenship	A	Housing	E
Discrimination	B	Gambling	F
Residence Requirements	C	Freedom of Religion	G
Civil Service Examinations	D		

2 (#1)

These referrals are numbered consecutively regardless of year. The first referral by a particular agency on citizenship, for example, would be designated A1, followed by A2, A3, etc.

If no reference is made in a question as to how many letters involving a certain subject or how many lawsuits have been referred by an agency, assume that it is the first.

For each question, choose the file designation which is MOST appropriate for filing the material described in the question.

1. In January 2010, two candidates in a 2009 civil service examination for positions with the Department of Correction filed a suit against the Department of Personnel seeking to set aside an educational requirement for the title.
   The Department of Personnel immediately referred the lawsuit to the legal office for handling.

   A. 1-9:1   B. 1-0:D1   C. 7-9:D1   D. 7-0:1

2. In 2014, the Police Department made its sixth request for an opinion on whether an employee assignment proposed for 2015 could be considered discriminatory.

   A. 2-5:1-B6   B. 2-4:6   C. 2-4:1-B6   D. 2-4:B6

3. In 2015, a lawsuit was brought by the Bay Island Action Committee against the Board of Estimate in which the plaintiff sought withdrawal of approval of housing for the elderly in the Bay Island area given by the Board in 2015.

   A. 8-3:1   B. 8-5:1   C. 8-3:B1   D. 8-5:E1

4. In December 2014, community leaders asked the Police Department to ban outdoor meetings of a religious group on the grounds that the meetings were disrupting the area. Such meetings had been held from time to time during 2014. On January 31, 2015, the Police Department asked the government legal office for an opinion on whether granting this request would violate the worshippers' right to freedom of religion.

   A. 2-4:G-1   B. 2-5:G1   C. 2-5:B-1   D. 2-4:B1

5. In 2014, a woman filed suit against the Board of Elections. She alleged that she had not been permitted to vote at her usual polling place in the 2013 election and had been told she was not registered there. She claimed that she had always voted there and that her record card had been lost. This was the fourth case of its type for this agency.

   A. 6-4:4   B. 6-3:C4   C. 3-4:6   D. 6-3:4

6. A lawsuit was brought in 2011 by the Ace Pinball Machine Company against the Commissioner of Consumer Affairs. The lawsuit contested an ordinance which banned the use of pinball machines on the ground that they are gambling devices.
   This was the third lawsuit to which the Department of Consumer Affairs was a party.

   A. 4-1:1   B. 4-3:F1   C. 4-1:3   D. 3F-4:1

7. You are instructed by your supervisor to type a statement that must be signed by the person making the statement and by three witnesses to the signature. The typed statement will take two pages and will leave no room for signatures if the normal margin is maintained at the bottom of the second page.
   In this situation, the PREFERRED method is to type

   A. the signature lines below the normal margin on the second page
   B. nothing further and have the witnesses sign without a typed signature line
   C. the signature lines on a third page
   D. some of the text and the signature lines on a third page

8. Certain legal documents always begin with a statement of venue - that is, the county and state in which the document is executed. This is usually boxed with a parentheses or colons.
   The one of the following documents that ALWAYS bears a statement of venue in a prominent position at its head is a(n)

   A. affidavit   B. memorandum of law
   C. contract of sale   D. will

9. A court stenographer is to take stenographic notes and transcribe the statements of a person under oath. The person has a heavy accent and speaks in ungrammatical and broken English.
   When he or she is transcribing the testimony, of the following, the BEST thing for them to do is to

   A. transcribe the testimony exactly as spoken, making no grammatical changes
   B. make only the grammatical changes which would clarify the client's statements
   C. make all grammatical changes so that the testimony is in standard English form
   D. ask the client's permission before making any grammatical changes

10. When the material typed on a printed form does not fill the space provided, a Z-ruling is frequently drawn to fill up the unused space.
    The MAIN purpose of this practice is to

    A. make the document more pleasing to the eye
    B. indicate that the preceding material is correct
    C. insure that the document is not altered
    D. show that the lawyer has read it

11. After you had typed an original and five copies of a certain document, some changes were made in ink on the original and were initialed by all the parties. The original was signed by all the parties, and the signatures were notarized.
    Which of the following should *generally* be typed on the copies BEFORE filing the original and the copies? The inked changes

    A. but not the signatures, initials, or notarial data
    B. the signatures and the initials but not the notarial data
    C. and the notarial data but not the signatures or initials
    D. the signatures, the initials, and the notarial data

12. The first paragraph of a noncourt agreement *generally* contains all of the following EXCEPT the

    A. specific terms of the agreement
    B. date of the agreement
    C. purpose of the agreement
    D. names of the parties involved

13. When typing an answer in a court proceeding, the place where the word ANSWER should be typed on the first page of the document is

    A. at the upper left-hand corner
    B. below the index number and to the right of the box containing the names of the parties to the action
    C. above the index number and to the right of the box containing the names of the parties to the action
    D. to the left of the names of the attorneys for the defendant

14. Which one of the following statements BEST describes the legal document called an acknowledgment?
    It is

    A. an answer to an affidavit
    B. a receipt issued by the court when a document is filed
    C. proof of service of a summons
    D. a declaration that a signature is valid

15. Suppose you typed the original and three copies of a legal document which was dictated by an attorney in your office. He has already signed the original copy, and corrections have been made on all copies.
    Regarding the copies, which one of the following procedures is the PROPER one to follow?

    A. Leave the signature line blank on the copies
    B. Ask the attorney to sign the copies
    C. Print or type the attorney's name on the signature line on the copies
    D. Sign your name to the copies followed by the attorney's initials

16. Suppose your office is defending a particular person in a court action. This person comes to the office and asks to see some of the lawyer's working papers in his file. The lawyer assigned to the case is out of the office at the time.
    You SHOULD

    A. permit him to examine his entire file as long as he does not remove any materials from it
    B. make an appointment for the caller to come back later when the lawyer will be there
    C. ask him what working papers he wants to see and show him only those papers
    D. tell him that he needs written permission from the lawyer in order to see any records

17. Suppose that you receive a phone call from an official who is annoyed about a letter from your office which she just received. The lawyer who dictated the letter is not in the office at the moment.
    Of the following, the BEST action for you to take is to

    A. explain that the lawyer is out but that you will ask the lawyer to return her call when he returns
    B. take down all of the details of her complaint and tell her that you will get back to her with an explanation
    C. refer to the proper file so that you can give her an explanation of the reasons for the letter over the phone
    D. make an appointment for her to stop by the office to speak with the lawyer

18. Suppose that you have taken dictation for an interoffice memorandum. You are asked to prepare it for distribution to four lawyers in your department whose names are given to you. You will type an original and make four copies. Which one of the following is CORRECT with regard to the typing of the lawyers' names?
    The names of all of the lawyers should appear

    A. *only* on the original
    B. on the original and each copy should have the name of one lawyer
    C. on each of the copies but not on the original
    D. on the original and on all of the copies

19. Regarding the correct typing of punctuation, the GENERALLY accepted practice is that there should be

    A. two spaces after a semi-colon
    B. one space before an apostrophe used in the body of a word
    C. no space between parentheses and the matter enclosed
    D. one space before and after a hyphen

20. Suppose you have just completed typing an original and two copies of a letter requesting information. The original is to be signed by a lawyer in your office. The first copy is for the files, and the second is to be used as a reminder to follow up.
    The PROPER time to file the file copy of the letter is

    A. after the letter has been signed and corrections have been made on the copies
    B. before you take the letter to the lawyer for his signature
    C. after a follow-up letter has been sent
    D. after a response to the letter has been received

21. A secretary in a legal office has just typed a letter. She has typed the copy distribution notation on the copies to indicate *blind copy distribution*. This *blind copy* notation shows that

    A. copies of the letter are being sent to persons that the addressee does not know
    B. copies of the letter are being sent to other persons without the addressee's knowledge
    C. a copy of the letter will be enlarged for a legally blind person
    D. a copy of the letter is being given as an extra copy to the addressee

22. Suppose that one of the attorneys in your office dictates material to you without indicating punctuation. He has asked that you give him, as soon as possible, a single copy of a rough draft to be triple-spaced so that he can make corrections.
Of the following, what is the BEST thing for you to do in this situation?

    A. Assume that no punctuation is desired in the material
    B. Insert the punctuation as you type the rough draft
    C. Transcribe the material exactly as dictated, but attach a note to the attorney stating your suggested changes
    D. Before you start to type the draft, tell the attorney you want to read back your notes so that he can indicate punctuation

23. When it is necessary to type a mailing notation such as CERTIFIED, REGISTERED, or FEDEX on an envelope, the GENERALLY accepted place to type it is

    A. directly above the address
    B. in the area below where the stamp will be affixed
    C. in the lower left-hand corner
    D. in the upper left-hand corner

24. When taking a citation of a case in shorthand, which of the following should you write FIRST if you are having difficulty keeping up with the dictation?

    A. Volume and page number   B. Title of volume
    C. Name of plaintiff   D. Name of defendant

25. All of the following abbreviations and their meanings are correctly paired EXCEPT

    A. viz. - namely   B. ibid. - refer
    C. n.b. - note well   D. q.v. - which see

KEY (CORRECT ANSWERS)

1.	D	11.	D
2.	D	12.	A
3.	B	13.	B
4.	B	14.	D
5.	A	15.	C
6.	C	16.	B
7.	D	17.	A
8.	A	18.	D
9.	A	19.	C
10.	C	20.	A

21.	B
22.	B
23.	B
24.	A
25.	B

EXAMINATION SECTION
TEST 1

DIRECTIONS: Each question or incomplete statement is followed by several suggested answers or completions. Select the one that BEST answers the question or completes the statement. *PRINT THE LETTER OF THE CORRECT ANSWER IN THE SPACE AT THE RIGHT.*

Questions 1-9.

DIRECTIONS: Questions 1 through 9 consist of sentences which may or may not be examples of good English usage. Consider grammar, punctuation, spelling, capitalization, awkwardness, etc. Examine each sentence, and then choose the correct statement about it from the four choices below it. If the English usage in the sentence given is better than it would be with any of the changes suggested in options B, C, and D, choose option A. Do not choose an option that will change the meaning of the sentence.

1. According to Judge Frank, the grocer's sons found guilty of assault and sentenced last Thursday. 1.____
    A. This is an example of acceptable writing.
    B. A comma should be placed after the word *sentenced*.
    C. The word *were* should be placed after *sons*
    D. The apostrophe in *grocer's* should be placed after the *s*.

2. The department heads assistant said that the stenographers should type duplicate copies of all contracts, leases, and bills. 2.____
    A. This is an example of acceptable writing.
    B. A comma should be placed before the word *contracts*.
    C. An apostrophe should be placed before the *s* in *heads*.
    D. Quotation marks should be placed before *the stenographers* and after *bills*.

3. The lawyers questioned the men to determine who was the true property owner? 3.____
    A. This is an example of acceptable writing.
    B. The phrase *questioned the men* should be changed to *asked the men questions*.
    C. The word *was* should be changed to *were*.
    D. The question mark should be changed to a period.

4. The terms stated in the present contract are more specific than those stated in the previous contract. 4.____
    A. This is an example of acceptable writing.
    B. The word *are* should be changed to *is*.
    C. The word *than* should be changed to *then*.
    D. The word *specific* should be changed to *specified*.

5. Of the lawyers considered, the one who argued more skillful was chosen for the job. 5.____
    A. This is an example of acceptable writing.
    B. The word *more* should be replaced by the word *most*.
    C. The word *skillful* should be replaced by the word *skillfully,*
    D. The word *chosen* should be replaced by the word *selected*.

7

6. Each of the states has a court of appeals; some states have circuit courts.   6._____

   A. This is an example of acceptable writing.
   B. The semi-colon should be changed to a comma.
   C. The word *has* should be changed to *have*.
   D. The word *some* should be capitalized.

7. The court trial has greatly effected the child's mental condition.   7._____

   A. This is an example of acceptable writing.
   B. The word *effected* should be changed to *affected*.
   C. The word *greatly* should be placed after *effected*.
   D. The apostrophe in *child's* should be placed after the *s*.

8. Last week, the petition signed by all the officers was sent to the Better Business Bureau.   8._____

   A. This is an example of acceptable writing.
   B. The phrase *last week* should be placed after *officers*.
   C. A comma should be placed after *petition*.
   D. The word *was* should be changed to *were*.

9. Mr. Farrell claims that he requested form A-12, and three booklets describing court procedures.   9._____

   A. This is an example of acceptable writing.
   B. The word *that* should be eliminated.
   C. A colon should be placed after *requested*.
   D. The comma after *A-12* should be eliminated.

Questions 10-21.

DIRECTIONS: Questions 10 through 21 contain a word in capital letters followed by four suggested meanings of the word. For each question, choose the BEST meaning for the word in capital letters.

10. SIGNATORY - A   10._____

    A. lawyer who draws up a legal document
    B. document that must be signed by a judge
    C. person who signs a document
    D. true copy of a signature

11. RETAINER - A   11._____

    A. fee paid to a lawyer for his services
    B. document held by a third party
    C. court decision to send a prisoner back to custody pending trial
    D. legal requirement to keep certain types of files

12. BEQUEATH - To   12._____

    A. receive assistance from a charitable organization
    B. give personal property by will to another
    C. transfer real property from one person to another
    D. receive an inheritance upon the death of a relative

13. RATIFY - To

    A. approve and sanction
    B. forego
    C. produce evidence
    D. summarize

14. CODICIL - A

    A. document introduced in evidence in a civil action
    B. subsection of a law
    C. type of legal action that can be brought by a plaintiff
    D. supplement or an addition to a will

15. ALIAS

    A. Assumed name
    B. In favor of
    C. Against
    D. A writ

16. PROXY - A(n)

    A. phony document in a real estate transaction
    B. opinion by a judge of a civil court
    C. document containing appointment of an agent
    D. summons in a lawsuit

17. ALLEGED

    A. Innocent
    B. Asserted
    C. Guilty
    D. Called upon

18. EXECUTE - To

    A. complete a legal document by signing it
    B. set requirements
    C. render services to a duly elected executive of a municipality
    D. initiate legal action such as a lawsuit

19. NOTARY PUBLIC - A

    A. lawyer who is running for public office
    B. judge who hears minor cases
    C. public officer, one of whose functions is to administer oaths
    D. lawyer who gives free legal services to persons unable to pay

20. WAIVE - To

    A. disturb a calm state of affairs
    B. knowingly renounce a right or claim
    C. pardon someone for a minor fault
    D. purposely mislead a person during an investigation

21. ARRAIGN - To

    A. prevent an escape
    B. defend a prisoner
    C. verify a document
    D. accuse in a court of law

Questions 22-40.

DIRECTIONS: Questions 22 through 40 each consist of four words which may or may not be spelled correctly. If you find an error in
only one word, mark your answer A;
any two words, mark your answer B;
any three words, mark your answer C;
none of these words, mark your answer D.

#	1	2	3	4
22.	occurrence	Febuary	privilege	similiar
23.	separate	transferring	analyze	column
24.	develop	license	bankrupcy	abreviate
25.	subpoena	arguement	dissolution	foreclosure
26.	exaggerate	fundamental	significance	warrant
27.	citizen	endorsed	marraige	appraissal
28.	precedant	univercity	observence	preliminary
29.	stipulate	negligence	judgment	prominent
30.	judisial	whereas	release	guardian
31.	appeal	larcenny	transcrip	jurist
32.	petition	tenancy	agenda	insurance
33.	superfical	premise	morgaged	maintainance
34.	testamony	publically	installment	possessed
35.	escrow	decree	eviction	miscelaneous
36.	securitys	abeyance	adhere	corporate
37.	kaleidoscope	anesthesia	vermilion	tafetta
38.	congruant	barrenness	plebescite	vigilance
39.	picnicing	promisory	resevoir	omission
40.	supersede	banister	wholly	seize

KEY (CORRECT ANSWERS)

1.	C	11.	A	21.	D	31.	B
2.	C	12.	B	22.	B	32.	D
3.	D	13.	A	23.	D	33.	C
4.	A	14.	D	24.	B	34.	B
5.	C	15.	A	25.	A	35.	A
6.	A	16.	C	26.	D	36.	A
7.	B	17.	B	27.	B	37.	A
8.	A	18.	A	28.	C	38.	B
9.	D	19.	C	29.	D	39.	C
10.	C	20.	B	30.	A	40.	D

EXAMINATION SECTION
TEST 1

DIRECTIONS: Each question or incomplete statement is followed by several suggested answers or completions. Select the one that BEST answers the question or completes the statement. *PRINT THE LETTER OF THE CORRECT ANSWER IN THE SPACE AT THE RIGHT.*

1. Which of the following is LEAST correct according to Article 375 V.T.L.? 1.____
   A. No vehicle shall be towed by a rope or other non-rigid connection which is longer than 16 feet.
   B. A motor vehicle being towed by a non-rigid connection must have a licensed driver in such motor vehicle who shall steer it when it is being towed.
   C. This rule (as in "B") does not apply in the counties of Nassau or Suffolk when a tractor is towing two trailers.
   D. The general rule is that a motor vehicle shall not be used to tow more than one other vehicle.

2. During daylight hours, when visibility for a distance of _____ feet ahead is not clear, a motor vehicle driven upon a public highway shall display its lights. 2.____
   A. 350   B. 500   C. 1,000   D. 100

3. Motor vehicles manufactured after 1/1/52 are required to display two rear red lamps during certain periods. These red lamps shall be visible from the rear for a distance of _____ feet. 3.____
   A. 500   B. 1,000   C. 350   D. 100

4. When a vehicle is required to display a number plate on the rear, a white light must be available to illuminate the number plate to make the numerals legible for at least _____ feet from the rear. 4.____
   A. 50   B. 75   C. 100   D. 350

5. Which of the following is LEAST correct concerning the use of colored and flashing lights? 5.____
   A. Green lights may be affixed to any motor vehicle owned by a volunteer ambulance worker.
   B. Blue lights may be affixed to motor vehicles owned by a member of a volunteer fire department.
   C. Amber lights may be used by hazard vehicles.
   D. Red lights or oscillating white lights may be used by either authorized emergency vehicles or by hazard vehicles.

6. Which of the following statements is LEAST correct concerning accident reports under Section 605 V.T.L.? 6.____
   A. An accident report is required whenever any person is killed or injured.
   B. An accident report is required whenever property damage to any one person exceeds $1000.

13

C. If the operator of the involved vehicle cannot make the report, then the owner should make it within 10 days after he learns the facts.
D. The report required shall be made in duplicate.

7. Every police or judicial officer to whom an accident resulting in injury to a person shall reported to the V.T.L., shall IMMEDIATELY investigate the facts, or cause the same to be investigated provided, however, that the report of the accident is made to the police officer or judicial officer within _____ days after such accident.

   A. 5   B. 10   C. 15   D. 20

7._____

8. Which of the following is LEAST correct concerning the requirement of stopping before passing or overtaking a stopped school bus in this state?

   A. The rule in a city is the same as the rule in the remainder of the state.
   B. If the stopped school bus does not have its red visual signal in operation, it may be passed or overtaken.
   C. If the school bus is stopped for the purpose of receiving or discharging any school children, and a red visual signal is in operation on said bus, then an overtaking or passing vehicle approaching from EITHER direction must be stopped before reaching the school bus.
   D. The driver of a vehicle stopped as per choice C above may not proceed until the school bus resumes motion.

8._____

9. Reckless driving means driving or using any motor vehicle, motorcycle, or any other vehicle propelled by any power other than muscular power or any appliance or accessory thereof in a manner which unreasonably interferes with the free and proper use of the public highway.
The above statement defines a

   A. traffic infraction
   B. misdemeanor
   C. violation
   D. petty offense
   E. felony if there has been a prior conviction within 18 months

9._____

10. Which of the following is MOST accurate according to 1195 of the V.T.L.?

   A. No person shall operate a motor vehicle while he has .10 of one percentum or more by weight of alcohol in his blood.
   B. Any person who operates a motor vehicle or motorcycle in this state shall be deemed to have given his consent to a chemical test of his breath, blood, urine, or saliva for the purpose of determining the alcoholic or drug content of his blood.
   C. Only a physician or a registered professional nurse, acting at the request of a police officer, shall be entitled to withdraw blood, urine, or saliva for the purpose of determining alcoholic or drug content.
   D. The person tested shall be permitted to have a physician of his own choosing administer a chemical test in addition to the one administered at the direction of the police officer.

10._____

11. Which of the following is LEAST accurate according to 1192 of the V.T.L.?   11._____

    A. Driving with .08% or more alcohol in the blood is a misdemeanor.
    B. A person who now stands convicted of A or B above and who has a prior conviction of either within ten years is guilty of a felony.
    C. Driving while ability to operate is impaired by drugs is a misdemeanor.
    D. A person who now stands convicted of D above and who has a prior conviction of A, B, or D above within 10 years is guilty of a felony.

12. Which of the following is LEAST accurate according to the V.T.L.?   12._____

    A. Driving while intoxicated is a misdemeanor.
    B. Driving with more than .08% alcohol in the blood is a misdemeanor.
    C. Driving while ability is impaired by the consumption of alcohol is a traffic infraction
    D. Driving while ability is impaired by drugs is a traffic infraction.

13. According to Section 116 of the V.T.L., a FLAMMABLE LIQUID is defined as a liquid which has a flash point of less than _____ degrees Fahrenheit.   13._____

    A. 70   B. 80   C. 60   D. 90

14. According to Section 125 of the V.T.L., which of the following would be considered to be a motor vehicle? A(n)   14._____

    A. motorcycle
    B. snow-mobile
    C. vehicle which runs only upon rails or track
    D. electrically driven invalid chair operated or driven by an invalid

15. Which of the following is LEAST correct according to the V.T.L.?   15._____

    A. The defined term "police officer" includes every duly designated peace officer acting pursuant to his special duties.
    B. The defined term "person" includes a corporation.
    C. A "pedestrian" is any person who is afoot.
    D. An "omnibus" is any vehicle used in the business of transporting people for hire which has a carrying capacity of more than 10 persons.

16. Which of the following would NOT be considered a "vehicle" as that term is defined in Section 159 of the V.T.L.? A(n)   16._____

    A. device used exclusively upon stationary rails or tracks
    B. motor-driven bicycle
    C. air-powered four-wheeled wagon
    D. horse being ridden

17. According to the V.T.L., the "parking area of a shopping center" is sometimes subject to the traffic control regulations of the V.T.L. Which of the following is MOST correct concerning the size of such parking area? It must be   17._____

    A. at least one acre
    B. at least 100 feet of business frontage
    C. at least 500 feet along a highway
    D. any size if the public has access and more than one business is serviced thereby

18. A "vanpool vehicle" is said to have a seating capacity, in addition to the driver, of   18.____

    A. not less than 6 nor more than 15 passengers
    B. not more than 10 passengers
    C. nine passengers
    D. ten passengers or less

19. P.O. Collins observes Sam drive through a red light and he "pulls him over." When Collins   19.____
    asks Sam for his license and registration, Collins sees actions which makes him think
    Sam was drinking. Collins asks Sam to submit to a breath test to determine if Sam has
    consumed alcohol. Sam submits and the test indicates that Sam has consumed alcohol,
    amount unknown. Collins' NEXT action should be to

    A. arrest Sam for violation of 1192 V.T.L.
    B. direct Sam to engage in coordination tests such as "finger to nose," "walking a
       straight line," etc.
    C. require Sam to submit to a chemical test as per 1194 of the V.T.L.
    D. release Sam if the amount of alcohol consumed, as indicated in the field breath
       test, is .05% or less

20. Which of the following statements concerning the court order to compel a chemical test   20.____
    is MOST accurate?

    A. Application may be made to the judge of any criminal court.
    B. Application must be made in person and in writing.
    C. When the order is issued, the chemical test may be administered even if the two
       hour time limit in Section 1194 has expired.
    D. If the defendant is unable to give his consent to a chemical test (unconscious), a
       court order may be obtained.

21. Which of the following substances is NOT listed in Section 1194 of the V.T.L. as a sub-   21.____
    stance which may be tested to determine blood alcohol content?

    A. Breath   B. Blood
    C. Urine   D. Perspiration

22. The chemical test authorized under Section 1194 of the V.T.L. must be administered at   22.____
    the direction of

    A. a police officer
    B. the judge of a criminal court
    C. a physician
    D. the desk officer

23. Persons who may be authorized to withdraw blood for the purpose of determining alco-   23.____
    holic content include
            I.   a physician
            II. a registered professional nurse
            III. any laboratory technician
            IV. a registered physician's assistant
    The CORRECT answer is:

    A. I, II   B. I, II, III
    C. I, II, IV   D. II, III, IV

24. Any person operating a motor vehicle that is involved in an accident resulting in death, injury, or property damage exceeding $1000 must report the accident to the Department of Motor Vehicles within _____ days.

   A. 7   B. 10   C. 20   D. 30

25. Article 140 of the C.P.L. contains the rules which govern "arrests without a warrant." These, however, are NOT the only arrest laws. The V.T.L. contains a "law of arrest" in Section 1193 that governs arrests without a warrant for violations of Section 1192 of the V.T.L. Consider the following statements regarding this "law of arrest" which may or may not be CORRECT:
   I. The police officer needs R.C.T.B. that the person to be arrested violated Section 1192.
   II. The violation of Section 1192 must in fact have been committed.
   III. The violation of Section 1192 need not have been committed in the arresting officer's presence if such violation is coupled with an accident or collision in which such person is involved.

   The choice below which most accurately describes which of the above statements is/are consistent with the provisions of Section 1193 V.T.L. is:

   A. I, II, III   B. II, III
   C. I, III   D. I, II

KEY (CORRECT ANSWERS)

1. C		11. D	
2. C		12. D	
3. A		13. B	
4. A		14. A	
5. D		15. D	
6. D		16. A	
7. A		17. A	
8. D		18. A	
9. B		19. C	
10. D		20. D	

21. D
22. A
23. C
24. B
25. A

TEST 2

DIRECTIONS: Each question or incomplete statement is followed by several suggested answers or completions. Select the one that BEST answers the question or completes the statement. *PRINT THE LETTER OF THE CORRECT ANSWER IN THE SPACE AT THE RIGHT.*

1. Which of the following are considered to be "Authorized Emergency Vehicles" under the V.T.L.? 1.____

    A. Ambulance, police and fire vehicles only
    B. Civil Defense emergency, police, fire and ambulance vehicles only
    C. All of the above plus utility company repair trucks
    D. All of C plus emergency ambulance service vehicles and ordinance disposal vehicles of U.S. Armed Forces

2. Which of the following defined terms is LEAST correct according to the V.T.L.? 2.____

    A. A "driver" means every person who operates or drives or is in actual physical control of a vehicle.
    B. The term "drug" as used in the V.T.L. includes depressant, stimulant, hallucinogenic and narcotic drugs.
    C. A "motorcycle" is a motor vehicle having a seat or saddle for the rider and designed to travel on not more than three wheels, any two of which are more than twenty inches in diameter.
    D. An "owner" of a vehicle does NOT include a lien holder.

3. According to Article 1 of the V.T.L., which of the following is LEAST correct? 3.____

    A. A bus includes every motor vehicle used for transporting persons and designed to carry more than seven passengers.
    B. An omnibus is any motor vehicle used in the business of transporting passengers for hire, except those used to transport agricultural workers to and from their employment.
    C. A snow-mobile is specifically excluded from the definition of a motor vehicle.
    D. Parking means the standing of a vehicle, whether occupied or not, except when done temporarily for the purpose of and while actually engaged in loading or unloading merchandise or passengers.

4. According to the V.T.L., a "business district" is defined as the territory contiguous to and including a highway when within 600 feet along such highway there are buildings in use for business or industrial purposes which occupy a certain amount of frontage along the highway. 4.____
Which of the following is MOST correct concerning the frontage along the highway? It must be

    A. at least 300 feet on both sides of the highway
    B. at least 600 feet collectively on both sides of the highway
    C. at least 300 feet on one side or 300 feet collectively on both sides
    D. a minimum of at least 150 feet on each side of the highway

5. Which of the following is LEAST correct according to the V.T.L.?

   A. A "traffic infraction" is a violation of any law regulating traffic which is NOT declared to be a felony or a misdemeanor.
   B. Punishment for a traffic infraction shall NOT be deemed a penal or criminal punishment.
   C. For purposes of arrest without a warrant, a traffic infraction shall be deemed an offense.
   D. Any fine imposed by an administrative tribunal for a traffic infraction shall NOT be a civil penalty.

6. According to Section 251 of the V.T.L., a member of the Armed Forces who has been issued an Operator's License by the Armed Forces may operate a motor vehicle upon the highways of the state WITHOUT being licensed under the V.T.L. for a period of _____ days after he has entered the state.

   A. 45   B. 30   C. 20   D. 60

7. According to Section 252 of the V.T.L., a temporary in-transit or transportation registration or permit issued by another state to the purchaser of a motor vehicle shall be valid only for a period of _____ days after the holder thereof has entered this state for the purpose of transporting the vehicle to the jurisdiction in which it will be regularly registered.

   A. 3   B. 5   C. 7   D. 10

8. Which of the following is LEAST accurate concerning required lights on motor vehicles?

   A. Two front lamps, one on each side, having light sources of equal power, shall be displayed from 1/2 hour after sunset to 1/2 hour before sunrise.
   B. The lamps referred to in A shall also be displayed at such other times when visibility for a distance of 1000 feet ahead of such motor vehicle is not clear.
   C. At least one lighted red lamp on the rear of such motor vehicle if manufactured before 1/1/52 visible for a distance of at least 500 feet shall be displayed during the times referred to in A and B.
   D. All motor vehicles shall be equipped with a white rear light which shall be lighted when, the ignition is energized and reverse gear is engaged.

9. According to Section 304b V.T.L., if a vehicle is inspected and found to be in need of repairs or adjustment, a period of _____ is allowed for the making of the repairs.

   A. 10 days   B. one week
   C. 15 days   D. one month

10. According to Section 306 of the V.T.L., which is LEAST accurate? A

    A. motor vehicle parked without a proper inspection certificate constitutes a parking violation
    B. person who unlawfully removes an inspection certificate from a vehicle is guilty of a traffic infraction
    C. person who makes a false inspection certificate is guilty of a misdemeanor
    D. person who displays on a motor vehicle an inspection certificate without an inspection having been made commits a misdemeanor

11. Which of the following is LEAST correct concerning items subject to inspection according to Article 301 V.T.L. dealing with periodic inspection of motor vehicles?

    A. Wheel alignment is included.
    B. The vehicle identification number is included.
    C. The odometer is not included.
    D. Lights, brakes, and steering are included.

12. If one is arrested and charged with "operating a motor vehicle while under the influence of alcohol or drugs" and evidence of the amount of alcohol in the defendant's blood is admitted, it would be MOST INACCURATE to state that

    A. .02 of one percent or less is prima facie evidence that defendant was neither impaired nor intoxicated
    B. more than .02 but not more than .04 of one percent is prima facie that defendant was not intoxicated but is not prima facie that he was impaired
    C. more than .04 but less than .08 of one percent is prima facie that defendant was not intoxicated but is prima facie that he was impaired
    D. .08 of one percent or less precludes a finding that defendant was guilty of driving while intoxicated

13. If one is arrested and charged under Section 1192 of the V.T.L., and convicted of same, the conviction may be for a felony if certain conditions are present. It would NOT result in such felony conviction if he is now charged with driving

    A. while intoxicated with a prior conviction for same within the preceding 10 years
    B. with .08 percent, or more, of alcohol in the blood with a prior conviction for same within the preceding 10 years
    C. with .08 percent, or more, of alcohol in the blood with a prior conviction for driving while intoxicated within the preceding 10 years
    D. while impaired by the use of a drug with a previous conviction of driving with .10 percent, or more, of alcohol in the blood within the preceding 10 years

14. Under the V.T.L., various tests may be administered to determine blood-alcohol content. Of the following, it would be MOST INACCURATE to state that

    A. every person operating a motor vehicle and who violates a provision of the V.T.L. may be requested to submit to a breath test
    B. one, properly arrested for violation of Section 1192 V.T.L., is deemed to have consented to a chemical test to determine his blood alcohol or drug content
    C. such test in C above must be administered at the direction of a police officer
    D. only a physician, or other specifically qualified person, may obtain blood, urine, or saliva samples for such test

15. According to the provisions of the V.T.L., in which of the following offenses would a second (or third) offense committed within 10 years amount to a felony?

    A. Reckless driving
    B. Third speed coupled with accident involving serious physical injury
    C. Leaving the scene of a physical injury accident
    D. Sale of a false certificate or registration

16. Under the provisions of the V.T.L., the percentage of blood alcohol which is to be given prima facie effect in determining that a person is neither intoxicated nor impaired is

    A. .02% or less
    B. .06% or .07%
    C. .08% or .09%
    D. less than .10%

17. A blood alcohol reading of .08% or .09% shall be given which of the following weights of evidence?

    A. Prima facie not intoxicated, but relevant regarding driving impaired
    B. Relevant regarding intoxication, but prima facie regarding driving impaired
    C. Prima facie not intoxicated, but prima facie impaired
    D. Relevant regarding both intoxication and driving impaired

18. The current charge and prior conviction within ten years, respectively, which will result in a felony charge according to the V.T.L. is:
    I. Driving impaired alcohol, driving impaired drugs
    II. Driving intoxicated, driving impaired alcohol
    III. Driving .10% or more blood alcohol, driving intoxicated
    IV. Driving impaired drugs, driving impaired drugs
    V. Driving intoxicated, driving impaired drugs
    VI. Driving intoxicated, driving .10% or more blood alcohol
    The CORRECT answer is:

    A. I, III, IV, VI
    B. III, IV, VI
    C. IV *only*
    D. all of the above

19. When a person refuses to submit to a chemical test after arrest for D.W.I., the report of said refusal shall be

    A. sent to the Commissioner of Motor Vehicles within 72 hours
    B. presented to the court upon arraignment of the defendant
    C. disclosed only if convicted of the offense
    D. sent to the Department of Motor Vehicles by the police agency involved so that a hearing may be scheduled

20. Following an arrest for D.W.I, and a refusal to submit to a chemical test, a court order may be issued directing the defendant to submit to the test when

    A. an accident involving property damage in excess of $1000 or personal injury has occurred
    B. the arrested person was the operator of the vehicle which was involved in an accident resulting in death or in serious injury to the operator or another person
    C. the arrested person was the operator of a vehicle which was involved in an accident resulting in death or serious injury to other than the operator
    D. an accident involving either death or physical injury has occurred

21. Boating accidents in which someone is killed or injured, or in which property damage exceeds $100.00, must be reported by the operator on a Boating Accident Report to the Office of Parks and Recreation within _____ days.

    A. 7
    B. 10
    C. 20
    D. 30

22. In the event of a snowmobile accident resulting in death, personal injury, or property damage in excess of $1000.00, a report must be prepared by the operator.
The CORRECT statement(s) regarding this report is(are):
   I. It must be filed within 7 days of the accident.
   II. It must be filed with the Office of Parks & Recreation.
   III. A copy of the report must be prepared for the sheriff of the county where the accident occurred.
The CORRECT answer is:

   A. I, II
   B. I, II, III
   C. I, III
   D. II, III

22.____

23. When you consider the sections of the V.T.L. that contain the blood alcohol percentages required for various D.W.I. offenses, which of the following would NOT be prima facie evidence that the person was impaired?

   A. .07%
   B. .05%
   C. .02%
   D. less than .10%

23.____

24. The definition which is INCONSISTENT with Article 10 of the R L. is that a

   A. "traffic infraction" means any offense defined as a "traffic infraction" by Section 155 of the V.T.L.
   B. "violation" means an offense for which a sentence to a term of imprisonment in excess of 15 days cannot be imposed
   C. "misdemeanor" means an offense for which a sentence to a term of imprisonment in excess of 15 days may be imposed, but for which a sentence to a term of imprisonment in excess of one year cannot be imposed
   D. "felony" means an offense for which a sentence to a term of imprisonment in excess of one year must be imposed

24.____

Questions 25 to 30.

DIRECTIONS: Each question consists of a statement. You are to indicate whether the statement is TRUE (T) or FALSE (F). *PRINT THE LETTER OF THE CORRECT ANSWER IN THE SPACE AT THE RIGHT*

25. According to the V.T.L., any police officer or peace officer acting pursuant to his official duties, can seize any motor vehicle or trailer when any original identification number or special identification number is destroyed, removed, altered, defaced, or covered.

25.____

26. Between ten and fifteen percent of reported auto thefts are fraudulent.

26.____

27. When vehicles are stolen in one state and recovered in another, the F.B.1, should be immediately notified because the interstate transportation of vehicles or aircraft known to be stolen is a federal felony.

27.____

28. Recovered stolen vehicles must be considered evidence and should be tagged, examined, and secured.

28.____

29. Upon satisfactory proof of ownership and payment of the reasonable and necessary expenses incurred in its preservation, the court in which the criminal action (if any) is pending MUST order the recovered vehicle to be delivered to the owner. 29._____

30. It is a Class E felony under the V.T.L. for any person-to sell or offer for sale a motor vehicle, trailer or part thereof which has a destroyed, removed, altered, defaced, or covered VIN or special identification number. 30._____

KEY (CORRECT ANSWERS)

1.	D	16.	A
2.	C	17.	C
3.	A	18.	B
4.	C	19.	B
5.	D	20.	C
6.	D	21.	A
7.	D	22.	B
8.	D	23.	C
9.	A	24.	D
10.	B	25.	T
11.	C	26.	T
12.	D	27.	T
13.	D	28.	T
14.	D	29.	F
15.	D	30.	T

EXAMINATION SECTION
TEST 1

DIRECTIONS: Each question or incomplete statement is followed by several suggested answers or completions. Select the one that BEST answers the question or completes the statement. *PRINT THE LETTER OF THE CORRECT ANSWER IN THE SPACE AT THE RIGHT.*

1. Leandra's Law, codified at 1192-2(b) is BEST defined as prohibiting driving 1.____
   A. while intoxicated
   B. while intoxicated with another person in the car
   C. while intoxicated with a child under the age of 15 in the car
   D. with a child under the age of 15 in the car

2. A DWAI violation is the abbreviation for driving 2.____
   A. while ability impaired
   B. while ability impugned
   C. with aggravated impairment
   D. while aggravated impairment

3. What is the blood alcohol level that, once reached or exceeded, definitely determines a violation of intoxication? 3.____
   A. .06   B. .07   C. .08   D. .09

Questions 4-6.

DIRECTIONS: Questions 4 through 6 are to be answered on the basis of the following fact pattern.

Three years ago, Jamal was convicted of driving while intoxicated and paid a fine of $350. After celebrating his co-worker's retirement at a local bar, Jamal is pulled over during a routine traffic stop and found, once again, to be operating a vehicle under the influence of alcohol.

4. What is the MAXIMUM fine Jamal may be ordered to pay? 4.____
   A. $300   B. $350   C. $500   D. $750

5. What is the MAXIMUM term of imprisonment Jamal may face and in what facility? 5.____
   A. 15 days, penitentiary or county jail
   B. 30 days, penitentiary or county jail
   C. 45 days, penitentiary or county jail
   D. 60 days, penitentiary or county jail

6. Assume that Jamal is convicted a third time of driving under the influence of alcohol. He will be found guilty of a 6.____
   A. violation
   B. misdemeanor
   C. felony
   D. aggravated assault

7. Which of the following may the court require as a condition for a sentence in violation of the Vehicle and Traffic Law?
   A. Attend a single session of the Victim Impact Program
   B. Recreate the scene of the crime
   C. Pay restitution directly to the victim's family, if one exists
   D. Permanent incarceration

7._____

8. Samantha is worried that her license may be suspended because she has driven without car insurance for over a year.
   Which of the following parties has the authority to revoke or suspend her license?
   A. County judge
   B. Superintendent of state police
   C. Commissioner of Motor Vehicles
   D. Any of the above

8._____

9. Katie was given an appearance ticket after she was caught driving over 120 miles per hour outside of Syracuse. Police Officer Lee believed he stumbled on a drag racing ring. Katie, however, never appeared in court.
   What is the likely punishment?
   A. Imprisonment for no less than three years
   B. Imprisonment for no less than five years
   C. Mandatory alcohol rehabilitation program
   D. Suspension for failure to answer an appearance ticket

9._____

Questions 10-11.

DIRECTIONS: Questions 10-11 are to be answered on the basis of the following fact pattern.

Daniel owed taxes for the 2014 tax year. He set up a payment plan with the New York Department of Taxation and Finance, but failed to make a single payment.

10. Pursuant to NYVTL, which of the following is the Commissioner of Taxation and Finance (or his or her agent) empowered to do?
    A. Suspend Daniel's license
    B. Place a metered tracker on Daniel's motor vehicle which will only allow Daniel to drive a mile or so in any direction before automatically powering down
    C. Revoke Daniel's car registration
    D. Ban anyone in Daniel's household from operating his car for personal or business use until the taxes are paid in full

10._____

11. After being contacted about his punishment for failure to pay taxes, Daniel sues the Commissioner of Taxation and Finance. Daniel alleges that because he is unable to drive his vehicle he cannot get to work and will lose his job.
    Is Daniel likely to prevail in a lawsuit against the Commissioner?

11._____

Daniel will
- A. be successful since he needs a car for work
- B. not be successful if he cannot prove his car is his only mode of transportation
- C. not be successful because he was put on notice he owed back taxes
- D. not be successful because the NYVTL specifically provides that no person shall right the right to commence a court action against the Commissioner for this purpose

Questions 12-14.

DIRECTIONS: Questions 12 through 14 are to be answered on the basis of the following fact pattern.

Ed knows that his friend Tom has had his license suspended at least ten times. Tom has failed to appear or pay for multiple tickets and each suspended license violation occurred on a different day. Tom asks to borrow Ed's car to drive from Buffalo to Brooklyn to visit his girlfriend, and Ed agreed.

12. What crime is Ed guilty of?
    Facilitating unlicensed operation of a
    - A. motorcycle
    - B. motor vehicle
    - C. motor vehicle as a misdemeanor
    - D. motor vehicle in the first degree

13. The LEAST Ed will pay in a fine is _____ in addition to a possible sentence of _____ and a term of imprisonment.
    - A. $1,000; probation
    - B. $2,000; probation
    - C. $3,000; probation
    - D. $5,000; restitution

14. The crime Ed is guilty of is classified as a
    - A. minor infraction
    - B. major infraction
    - C. Class A felony
    - D. Class E felony

15. Amy's brother, Bob, was visiting her in Hudson. He parked his SUV in a no standing zone and his car was towed. Amy attempted to get the car released, but she did not have the proper documentation to do so. An impounded vehicle shall not be released unless the person who redeems it furnishes satisfactory evidence of _____ and financial security.
    - A. license
    - B. rehabilitation
    - C. registration
    - D. insurance

16. Police officers saw Travis selling drugs out of his car. After Travis was arrested, his car was impounded. Travis's car was initially held as evidence, but the assistant district attorney no longer needs the car as evidence. Travis wants to claim his car, but the car cannot be released until he presents a(n)
    - A. affidavit from the arresting officers
    - B. release from the assistant district attorney
    - C. sworn testimony from the alleged drug buyers
    - D. bail bond

17. Aggravated failure to answer appearance tickets or pay fines will be imposed on a person who has at least _____ separate suspensions, imposed on at least _____ separate dates.
    A. 10; 20 B. 20; 20 C. 15; 15 D. 15; 20

17.____

18. Assume that Natalie is convicted of aggravated failure to answer appearance tickets or pay fines.
    What is her MAXIMUM possible punishment?
    A. Fine of $500, imprisonment of 180 days, or both
    B. Fine of $100, imprisonment of one year, or both
    C. Fine of $500 only
    D. Fine of imprisonment of 180 days only

18.____

Questions 19-20.

DIRECTIONS: Questions 19 and 20 are to be answered on the basis of the following fact pattern.

Robert has let his daughter, Veronica, borrow his car, even though he knew Veronica's license was suspended. She was only driving a short distance and promised to be home in a half hour. Instead, Veronica was pulled over and arrested for driving with a suspended license.

19. What type of crime has Robert committed?
    A. Felony   B. Serious traffic infraction
    C. Traffic infraction   D. Misdemeanor

19.____

20. Assuming that Robert continues to allow Veronica to borrow his car, even though her license remains suspended, Robert is availing himself of which of the following crimes?
    Facilitating aggravated unlicensed operation of a motor
    A. vehicle   B. vehicle in the second degree
    C. vehicle with felonious intent   D. vehicle with aggravated intent

20.____

Questions 21-22.

DIRECTIONS: Questions 21 and 22 are to be answered on the basis of the following fact pattern.

Dave failed to renew his medical certification for his commercial driver's license (CDL).

21. Within sixty days of Dave's certification status being changed to "non-certified," the Commissioner will do which of the following?
    A. Revoke Dave's CDL completely.
    B. Downgrade Dave's CDL to a learner's permit.
    C. Downgrade Dave's CDL to a non-commercial driver's license.
    D. Suspend Dave's license indefinitely.

21.____

22. Suppose that Dave simply forgot to submit the required medical variance documentation at the intervals imposed by law.
What will the consequences be?
 A. Dave's license will still be revoked.
 B. Dave's license will still be suspended indefinitely.
 C. Dave will be able to retain his CDL but on a part-time basis.
 D. The Commissioner will follow the same action as if the certification was not renewed.

23. Adam is charged with operating a commercial vehicle without a CDL. Adam claims that he has a CDL, but neglected to carry it with him at the time he was arrested.
What must Adam produce evidence that he had a valid CDL in order to be dismissed of the charges?
 A. Before his appearance in court
 B. Before the trial begins
 C. Before an attorney is selected
 D. Before the charges are finalized

24. Peter was convicted of homicide arising out of operation of a motor vehicle in Georgia.
Can Peter's license in his home state of New York, which was obtained before he moved to Georgia, be revoked?
 A. No, because he is a Georgia resident and his New York license is unaffected
 B. No, because the incident did not occur in New York
 C. Yes, because Peter is a New York native
 D. Yes

25. Emily approached a busy traffic intersection and discovered that traffic agents were directing traffic because the light was out. Emily became enraged that the traffic agents were not allowing her to make a right turn. Emily exited her vehicle and attacked the traffic enforcement agent. Emily was convicted of assault in the third degree.
Emily's license will be suspended for a period of not less than _____ days or more than _____ days.
 A. 30; 60
 B. 45; 60
 C. 30; 180
 D. 60; 180

KEY (CORRECT ANSWERS)

1.	C	11.	D
2.	A	12.	D
3.	C	13.	A
4.	D	14.	D
5.	B	15.	C
6.	B	16.	B
7.	A	17.	B
8.	D	18.	A
9.	D	19.	C
10.	A	20.	B

21. C
22. D
23. A
24. D
25. C

EXAMINATION SECTION
TEST 1

DIRECTIONS: Each question or incomplete statement is followed by several suggested answers or completions. Select the one that BEST answers the question or completes the statement. *PRINT THE LETTER OF THE CORRECT ANSWER IN THE SPACE AT THE RIGHT.*

Questions 1-9.

DIRECTIONS: Questions 1 through 9, inclusive, are based on the STATE MOTOR VEHICLE BUREAU'S POINT SYSTEM given below. Read this point carefully before answering these items.

STATE MOTOR VEHICLE BUREAU'S POINT SYSTEM

The newly revised point system was effective April 1. After that date, a driver having offenses resulting in an accumulation of eight points within two years, ten points within three years, or twelve points within four years, is to be summoned for a hearing which may result in the loss of his license. Under the point system, three points are charged for speeding, two points for passing a red light or crossing a double line or failing to stop at a stop sign, one and a half points for inoperative horn or insufficient lights, and one point for improper turn or failure to notify Bureau of change of address. The Commissioner of Motor Vehicles is required to revoke a driver's license if he has three speeding violations in a period of 18 months, or drives while intoxicated or leaves the scene of an accident or makes a false statement in his application for a driver's license. This system is necessary because studies show violations of traffic laws cause four out of five fatal accidents in the state.

1. The traffic offense which calls for license revocation if repeated three times within a period of 1½ years is
   A. passing a red light
   B. passing a stop sign
   C. crossing a double line
   D. speeding

2. The individual who has the power to revoke a driver's license is the
   A. traffic officer
   B. motor vehicle inspector
   C. Commissioner of Motor Vehicles
   D. Traffic Commissioner

3. Crossing a double line has a penalty of twice as many points as for
   A. making an improper turn
   B. speeding
   C. passing a red light
   D. an inoperative horn

4. Failure of a driver to properly notify the Bureau of Motor Vehicles of a change in his address carries a penalty of _____ point(s).
   A. ½   B. 1   C. 1½   D. 2

5. The point system is specifically designed to penalize the driver who
   A. is inexperienced
   B. repeatedly violates traffic laws
   C. is overage
   D. ignores parking violations

6. A false statement on a driver's license application calls for a penalty of 6.____
   A. 10 points B. 8 points
   C. license suspension D. license revocation

7. Insufficient lights carries a penalty of _____ point(s). 7.____
   A. ½ B. 1 C. 1½ D. 2

8. A driver is summoned for a hearing if, within a period of three years, he accumulates _____ points. 8.____
   A. 6 B. 8 C. 10 D. 12

9. The percentage of fatal accidents caused by traffic violations is 9.____
   A. 80% B. 70% C. 60% D. 50%

Questions 10-11.

DIRECTIONS: Questions 10 and 11 are to be answered ONLY according to the information given in the following passage.

The State Vehicle and Traffic law was changed effective October 1, 2005 to provide for all new driving licenses to be issued on a six-month probationary basis. The probationary license will be cancelled if during this six-month period the driver is found guilty of tailgating, speeding, reckless driving, or driving while his ability is impaired by alcohol. The license will also be cancelled if the driver is found guilty of two other moving violations. If a probationary license is cancelled, the driver must wait for sixty days after the date of cancellation before applying for another license; and if the application is approved, the applicant must meet certain additional requirements including a new road test before a new license will be issued.

10. It is MOST reasonable to assume that the main purpose of the change in the law referred to above was to 10.____
    A. find out who is responsible for most traffic accidents
    B. make the road tests more difficult for new drivers to pass
    C. make it harder to get a driver's license
    D. serve as a further check on the competence of new drivers

11. According to the above passage, we may assume that a probationary license will NOT be cancelled if a driver is found guilty of 11.____
    A. passing a red light and failing to keep to the right on a road
    B. following another vehicle too closely
    C. overtime parking at a meter on two or more occasions
    D. driving at 60 miles an hour on a road where the speed limit is 50 miles an hour

Questions 12-13.

DIRECTIONS: Questions 12 and 13 are to be answered ONLY on the basis of the following passage.

If a motor vehicle fails to pass inspection, the owner will be given a rejection notice by the inspection station. Repairs must be made within ten days after this notice is issued. It is not necessary to have the required adjustment or repairs made at the station where the inspection occurred. The vehicle may be taken to any other garage. Re-inspection after repairs may be made at any official inspection station, not necessarily the same station which made the initial inspection. The registration of any motor vehicle for which an inspection sticker has not been obtained as required, or which is not repaired and inspected within ten days after inspection indicates defects, is subject to suspension. A vehicle cannot be used on public highways while its registration is under suspension.

12. According to the above passage, the owner of a car which does NOT pass inspection must
    A. have repairs made at the same station which rejected this car
    B. take the car to another station and have it re-inspected
    C. have repairs made anywhere and then have the car re-inspected
    D. not use the car on a public highway until the necessary repairs have been made

13. According to the above passage, the one of the following which may be cause for suspension of the registration of a vehicle is that
    A. an inspection sticker was issued before the rejection notice had been in force for ten days
    B. it was not re-inspected by the station that rejected it originally
    C. it was not re-inspected either by the station that rejected it originally or by the garage which made the repairs
    D. it has not had defective parts repaired within ten days after inspection

Questions 14-18.

DIRECTIONS: Questions 14 through 18 are to be answered ONLY on the basis of the following passage.

Under the Vehicular Responsibility Law of a certain state, an insurance carrier who has previously furnished the Division of Roads and Vehicles with evidence of a vehicle registrant's financial responsibility (Form VR-1, VR-1A, VR-2B or VR-11) must, in case of termination of insurance, first notify the insured registrant at least 10 days in advance if the termination is due to failure to pay the insurance premium and at least 20 days if the termination is due to any other reason. The insurance carrier must then notify the Division not later than 30 days following the effective date of actual termination of insurance coverage. The only acceptable proof of such termination is Form VR-4.

Upon receipt of Form VR-4 by the Division, a search will be made for any superseding coverage or a record of voluntary surrender of plates and registration certificate on or prior to the effective date of termination. If such a record is found, no further action is taken by the

4 (#1)

Division. If the Division finds no record of acceptable superseding coverage or timely surrender of plates and registration, Form Letter VR-7T is sent to the registrant with a photostatic copy of Form VR-4, providing him with an opportunity to invalidate the proceeding to cancel his registration by submitting additional evidence, which may take the form of proof of continuous financial responsibility, timely sale of the vehicle, or evidence of voluntary surrender of plates and registration certificate. Only after the registrant has failed to comply by one of the above three methods is an order to cancel registration (Form VR-8) issued.

Upon the issuance of a cancellation order, a copy of the order is mailed to the registrant directing him to immediately surrender his plates and registration certificate to a specified area office of the Division. At the same time, two copies of the cancellation order are sent to the area office, where they are held for 15 days. If the registrant complies with the order, he is issued a notice of compliance (Form VR-3). If he fails to comply within the 15 days, two more copies of the order are mailed to the Highway Patrol for enforcement of the cancellation order. No further action is taken for a period of 30 days. If no record of enforcement is received, another copy of the cancellation order is sent to the Police Department as a follow-up.

14. When the Division of Roads and Vehicles receives acceptable evidence that the insurance coverage on a particular registrant has been terminated, it is required FIRST to 14.____
    A. cancel the registration if the insurance was terminated because of failure to pay the insurance premium
    B. notify the registrant to voluntarily surrender his plates and registration certificate on or prior to a certain date
    C. determine whether the registrant has obtained other insurance for that vehicle
    D. send the registrant Form Letter VR-7T stating that he must submit evidence to prevent cancellation of his registration

15. In order to comply with the above procedure, the MINIMUM number of copies of the cancellation order that must be prepared, including one to be kept in the central Division of Roads and Vehicles file, is 15.____
    A. 3   B. 4   C. 5   d. 6

16. The one of the following which is required before steps 16.____
    A. the insurance carrier to notify the Division of Roads and Vehicles in writing (VR-11) that the insured registrant's premium payment is 30 days overdue
    B. the registrant to notify the Division of Roads and Vehicles that he either intends to sell or has sold his vehicle
    C. Form VR-8 to be sent to the insured registrant by the Division of Roads and Vehicles
    D. Form VR-4 to be sent by the insurance carrier to the Division of Roads and Vehicles

17. The MAXIMUM amount of time a vehicle registrant is allowed in which to comply with a cancellation order before the police are asked to enforce the order is _____ days. 17.____
    A. 30   B. 35   C. 40   D. 45

18. It would be MOST accurate to state with regard to the issuance of a certificate 18.____
of compliance that the
    A. Division of Roads and Vehicles issues one to the registrant after he has submitted the additional evidence in response to Form Letter VR-7T
    B. Division of Roads and Vehicles may issue one to the registrant at any time after he has been mailed a copy of the cancellation order and before the Highway Patrol is notified
    C. Highway Patrol may issue one to the registrant if he surrenders his plates and registration to them during the 30 days following their receipt of the request for enforcement
    D. Highway Patrol may issue one to the registrant at any time before the Police Department is notified

Questions 19-22.

DIRECTIONS: Questions 19 through 22 are to be answered ONLY on the basis of the information given in the following passage.

All automotive accidents, no matter how slight, are to be reported to the Safety Division by the employee involved on Accident Report Form S-23 in duplicate. When the accident is of such a nature that it requires the filling out of the State Motor Vehicle Report Form MV-104, this form is also prepared by the employee in duplicate and sent to the Safety Division for comparison with Form S-23. The Safety Division forwards both copies of Form MV-104 to the Corporation Counsel, who sends one copy to the State Bureau of Motor Vehicles. When the information on the Form S-23 indicates that the employee may be at fault, an investigation is made by the Safety Division. If this investigation shows that the employee was at fault, the employee's dispatcher is asked to file a complaint on Form D-11. The foreman of mechanics prepares a damage report on Form D8 and an estimate of the cost of repairs on Form D-9. The dispatcher's complaint, the damage report, the repair estimate, and the employee's previous accident record are sent to the Safety Division where they are studied together with the accident report. The Safety Division then recommends whether or not disciplinary action should be taken against the employee.

19. According to the above passage, the Safety Division should be notified 19.____
whenever an automotive accident has occurred by means of Form(s)
    A. S-23
    B. S-23 and MV-104
    C. S-23, MV-104, D-8, D-9, and D-11
    D. S-23, MV-104, D-8, D-9, D-11, and employee's accident report

20. According to the above passage, the forwarding of the Form MV-104 to the 20.____
State Bureau of Motor Vehicles is done by the
    A. Corporation Counsel
    B. dispatcher
    C. employee involved in the accident
    D. Safety Division

21. According to the above passage, the Safety Division investigates an automotive accident if the
    A. accident is serious enough to be reported to the State Bureau of Motor Vehicles
    B. dispatcher files a complaint
    C. employee appears to have been at fault
    D. employee's previous accident report is poor

21.____

22. Of the forms mentioned in the above passage, the dispatcher is responsible for preparing the
    A. accident report form
    B. complaint form
    C. damage report
    D. estimate cost of repairs

22.____

Questions 23-25.

DIRECTIONS: Questions 23 through 25 are to be answered ONLY on the basis of the information given in the following passage.

One of the major problems in the control of city motor equipment, and especially passenger equipment, is keeping the equipment working for the city and for the city alone for as many hours of the day as is practical. Even when most city employees try to get the most out of the cars, a poor system of control will result in wasted car hours. Some city employees have a legitimate use for a car all day long while others use a car only a small part of the day and then let it stand. As a rule, trucks are easier to control than passenger cars because they are usually assigned to a specific job where a foreman continually oversees them. Even though trucks are usually fully utilized, there are times when the normal work assignment cannot be carried out because of weather conditions or seasonal changes. At such times, a control system could plan to make the trucks available for other uses.

23. According to the above passage, a problem connected with controlling the use of city motor equipment is
    A. increasing the life span of the equipment
    B. keeping the equipment working all hours of the day
    C. preventing the overuse of the equipment to avoid breakdowns
    D. preventing the private use of the equipment

23.____

24. According to the above passage, a good control system for passenger equipment will MOST likely lead to
    A. better employees being assigned to operate the cars
    B. fewer city employees using city cars
    C. fewer wasted car hours for city cars
    D. insuring that city cars are used for legitimate purposes

24.____

25. According to the above passage, a control system for trucks is useful because
    A. a foreman usually supervises each job
    B. special conditions sometimes prevent the planned use of a truck
    C. trucks are easier to control than passenger cars
    D. trucks are usually assigned to specific jobs where they cannot be fully utilized

25.____

Question 26.

DIRECTIONS: Question 26 is to be answered SOLELY on the basis of the following passage.

Whereas automobile travel in general corresponds to the general motor vehicles index, as represented by total gas usage. Traffic trends on one particular road may vary from average. Comparison of the records of various main arteries indicates that automobile travel on some highways has gone up much faster than the general trend of gas usage. The conclusion is that the bulk of local travel remains stable, but a very large share of the total increase in travel is concentrated on main highways. This would be especially true on new highways which provide better means of travel and foster trips which would not have been made if the new route has not been constructed.

26. According to the above passage, which one of the following is MOST likely to result in increased automobile travel?
    A. A new roadway
    B. Stable local conditions
    C. A choice of routes
    D. Traffic trends

26._____

Questions 27-30.

DIRECTIONS: Questions 27 through 30 are to be answered ONLY on the basis of the following passage.

Analysis of current data reveals that motor vehicle transportation actually requires less space than was used for other types of transportation in the pre-automobile era, even including the substantial area taken by freeways. The reason is that when the fast-moving through traffic is put on built-for-the-purpose arterial roads, then the amount of ordinary space needed for strictly local movement and for access to property drops sharply. Even the amount of land taken for urban expressways turns out to be surprisingly small in terms either of total urban acreage or of the volume of traffic they carry. No existing or contemplated urban expressway system requires as much as 3 percent of the land in the areas it serves, and this would be exceptionally high. The Los Angeles freeway system, when complete, will occupy only 2 percent of the available land; the same is true of the District of Columbia, where only 0.75 percent will be pavement, with the remaining 1.25 percent as open space. California studies estimate that, in a typical California urban community, 1.6 to 2 percent of the area should be devoted to freeways, which will handle 50 to 60 percent of all traffic needs, and about ten time as much land to the ordinary roads and streets that carry the rest of the traffic. By comparison, when John A. Sutter laid out Sacramento in 1850, he provided 38 percent of the area for street and sidewalks. The French architect, Pierre L'Enfant, proposed 59 percent of the area of the District of Columbia for roads and streets; urban renewal in Southwest Washington, incorporating a modern street network, reduced the acreage of space for pedestrian and vehicular traffic in the renewal area from 48.2 to 41.5 percent of the total. If we are to have a reasonable consideration of the impact of highway transportation on contemporary urban development, it would be well to understand these relationships.

27. The author of this passage says that
    A. modern transportation uses less space than was used for transportation before the auto age
    B. expressways require more space than streets in terms of urban acreage
    C. typical urban communities were poorly designed in terms of relationship between space used for traffic and that used for other purposes
    D. the need for local and access roads would increase if the number of expressways were increased

28. According to the above passage, it was originally planned that the percent of the area to be used for roads and streets in the District of Columbia should be MOST NEARLY
    A. 40%   B. 45%   C. 50%   D. 60%

29. The above passage states that the amount of space needed for local traffic
    A. *increases* when arterial highways are constructed
    B. *decreases* when arterial highways are constructed
    C. *decreases* when there is more land available
    D. *increases* when there is more land available

30. According to the above passage, studies estimate that, land devoted to in a typical California urban community, the amount of ordinary roads and streets as compared with that devoted to freeways should be MOST NEARLY as much.
    A. One-half   B. One-tenth   C. Twice   D. Ten times

KEY (CORRECT ANSWERS)

1.	D	11.	C	21.	C
2.	C	12.	C	22.	B
3.	A	13.	D	23.	D
4.	B	14.	C	24.	C
5.	B	15.	B	25.	B
6.	D	16.	D	26.	A
7.	C	17.	D	27.	A
8.	C	18.	B	28.	D
9.	A	19.	A	29.	B
10.	D	20.	A	30.	D

TEST 2

DIRECTIONS: Each question or incomplete statement is followed by several suggested answers or completions. Select the one that BEST answers the question or completes the statement. *PRINT THE LETTER OF THE CORRECT ANSWER IN THE SPACE AT THE RIGHT.*

Questions 1-5.

DIRECTIONS: Questions 1 through 5 are to be answered ONLY on the basis of information given in the following passage.

    Fatigue can make a driver incompetent. He may become less vigilant. He may lose judgment as to the speed and distance of other cars. His reaction time is likely to be slowed down, and he is less able to resist glare. With increasing fatigue, driving efficiency falls. Finally, nodding at the wheel results, from which accidents follow almost invariably.

    Accidents that occur with the driver asleep at the wheel are generally very serious. With the driver unconscious, no effort is made either to prevent the accident or to lessen its seriousness. Accidents increase as day wears on and reach their peak in the early evening and during the first half of the night. Driver fatigue undoubtedly plays a significant part in causing these frequent night accidents.

1. Among the results of fatigue, the passage does NOT indicate
   A. lessened hearing effectiveness
   B. lessened vigilance
   C. loss of driving efficiency
   D. increased reaction time

2. According to the passage, accidents almost always follow as a result of
   A. fatigue
   B. slowed down reaction time
   C. nodding at the wheel
   D. lessened vigilance

3. According to the passage, accidents that occur in the early evening and during the first half of the night are
   A. always caused by driver fatigue
   B. very frequently the result of lessened resistance to glare
   C. usually due to falling asleep at the wheel
   D. more frequent than accidents in the afternoon

4. According to the passage, very serious accidents result from
   A. falling asleep at the wheel
   B. poor driving
   C. lack of judgment
   D. poor vision

5. Referring to the passage, which of the following conclusions is NOT correct?
   A. There are only two paragraphs in the entire passage.
   B. One paragraph contains four sentences.
   C. There are six words in the first sentence.
   D. There is no sentence of less than six words.

Questions 6-8.

DIRECTIONS: Questions 6 through 8 are to be answered ONLY according to the information given in the following passage.

Drivers and pedestrians face additional traffic hazards during the fall months. Changing autumn weather conditions, longer hours of darkness, and the abrupt nightfall during the evening rush hour can mean more traffic deaths and injuries unless drivers and pedestrians exercise greater care and alertness. Drivers must adjust to changing light conditions; they cannot use the same driving habits and attitudes at dusk as they do during daylight. Moderate speed and continual alertness are imperative for safe city driving at this time of year.

6. According to the above passage, two new traffic risks which motorists face in the fall are
   A. changing weather conditions and more traffic during the evening rush hour
   B. fewer hours of daylight and sudden nightfall
   C. less care by pedestrians and a change in autumn weather conditions
   D. more pedestrians on the street and longer hours of darkness

6.____

7. According to the above passage, there may be more traffic deaths and injuries in the fall MAINLY because both pedestrians and drivers are
   A. distracted by car lights being turned on earlier
   B. hurrying to get home from work in the evening
   C. confronted with more traffic dangers
   D. using the streets in greater numbers

7.____

8. According to the above passage, an ESSENTIAL requirement of driving safely in the city in the fall is
   A. eyes down on the road at all times
   B. very slow speed
   C. no passing
   D. reasonable speed

8.____

Questions 9-11.

DIRECTIONS: Questions 9 through 11 are to be answered ONLY according to the information given in the following passage.

A traffic sign is a device mounted on a fixed or portable support through which a specific message is conveyed by means of words or symbols. It is erected through which a specific purpose of regulating, warning, or guiding traffic.

A regulatory sign is used to indicate the required method of traffic movement or the permitted use of a highway. It gives notice of traffic regulations that apply only at specific places or at specific times that would not otherwise be apparent.

A warning sign is used to call attention to conditions on or near a road that are actually or potentially hazardous to the safe movement of traffic.

A guide sign is used to direct traffic along a route or toward a destination, or to give directions, distances, or information concerning places or points of interest.

9. According to the above passage, which one of the following is NOT a *regulatory* sign?
   A. Right turn on red signal permitted
   B. Trucks use right lane
   C. Slippery when wet
   D. Speed limit 60

10. According to the above passage, which one of the following LEAST fits the description of a *warning* sign?
    A. No right turn
    B. Falling rock zone
    C. Low clearance, 12 ft. 6 in.
    D. Merging traffic

11. According to the above passage, which one of the following messages is LEAST likely to be conveyed by a *guide* sign?
    A. Southbound
    B. Signal ahead
    C. Bridge next exit
    D. Entering city

Questions 12-14.

DIRECTIONS: Questions 12 through 14 are to be answered ONLY on the basis of the information given in the following passage.

A National Safety Council study of 685,000 traffic accidents reveals that most accidents happen under *safe* conditions—in clear, dry weather, on straight roads, and when traffic volumes are low. The point is most accidents can be attributed to lapses on the part of the drivers rather than traffic or road conditions or deliberate law violations. Most drivers try to avoid accidents. Why, then, do so many get into trouble? A major cause is the average motorist's failure to recognize a hazard soon enough to avoid it entirely. He does not, by habit, notice the clues that are there for him to see. He takes constant risks in traffic without even knowing it. These faulty seeing habits plus the common distractions that all drivers must deal with, such as hurry, worry daydreaming, impatience, concentration on route problems, add up to a guaranteed answer—an accident.

12. According to a study by the National Safety Council, MOST accidents can be blamed on
    A. curving, hilly roads
    B. errors made by drivers
    C. heavy streams of traffic
    D. wet, foggy weather

13. According to the above passage, an IMPORTANT reason why the average motorist gets into an accident is that he
    A. does not see the danger of an accident soon enough
    B. does not try to avoid accidents
    C. drives at too great a speed
    D. purposely takes reckless chances

14. According to the above passage, it is NOT reasonable to say that drivers are distracted from their driving and possibly involved in an accident because they
    A. are impatient about something
    B. concentrate on the road ahead
    C. hurry to get to where they are going
    D. worry about some problem

14.____

Questions 15-18.

DIRECTIONS: Questions 15 through 18 are to be answered ONLY on the basis of the information given in the following passage.

If a good automobile road map is studied thoroughly before a trip is started, much useful information can be learned. This information may help to decrease the cost of and the time required for the trip and, at the same time, increase the safety and comfort of the trip. The legend found on the face of the map explains symbols and markings and the kind of roads on various routes. The legend also explains how to tell by width, color, or type of line whether the road is dual- or multiple-lane, and whether it is paved, all-weather, graded, earth, under construction, or proposed for construction. Federal routes are usually shown by a number within a shield, and state routes by a number within a circle. The legend also shows scale of miles on a bar marked to indicate the distance each portion of the bar represents on the earth's surface. Distances between locations on the map are shown by plain numerals beside the route lines; they indicate mileage between marked points or intersections. Add the mileage numbers shown along a route to determine distances.

15. According to the above passage, the markings on the road map will show
    A. a different color for a road proposed for construction than for one under construction
    B. a double line if a road is a dual-lane road
    C. what part of a road is damaged or being repaired
    D. which roads on state routes have more than two lanes

15.____

16. The above passage does NOT mention as a possible advantage of studying a good road map before beginning a trip the
    A. increase in interest of the trip
    B. reduction in the chance of an accident on the trip
    C. saving of money
    D. saving of time

16.____

17. According to the above passage, in order to find the total mileage of a certain route, a motorist should add the numbers
    A. on the bar scale in the legend
    B. between marked points beside the route lines
    C. inside a shield along the route
    D. within a circle along the route

17.____

18. According to the above passage, the legend on a road map includes information   18.____
    which a motorist could use to
    A. choose the best paved route
    B. figure the toll charges
    C. find the allowable speed limits
    D. learn the location of bridges

Questions 19-30.

DIRECTIONS: The following is an accident report similar to those used by departments for reporting accidents. Questions 19 through 30 are to be answered ONLY on the basis of the information contained in this accident report.

ACCIDENT REPORT

Date of Accident: April 12, ____
Place of Accident: 17th Ave. & 22nd St.
Time of Accident: 10:15 A.M.
City Vehicle:
Operator's Name: John Smith
Title: Motor Vehicle Operator
Badge No.: 17-5427
Operator License No.: S2874-7513-3984
Vehicle Code No.: B7-8213
License Plate No.: BK-4782
Damage to Vehicle: Left front fender dented; broken left front headlight and parking light; windshield wipers not operating

Date of Report: April 15, _____ Friday
Vehicle No. 2:
Operator's Name: James Jones
Operator's Address: 427 E. 198th St.
Operator License No.: J0837-0882-7851
Owner's Name: Michael Greene
Owner's Address: 582 E. 92nd St.
License Plate No.: 6Y-3916
Damage to Vehicle: Left front bumper bent inward; broken left front headlight; grille broken in three places

DESCRIPTION OF ACCIDENT: I was driving on 17th Avenue, a southbound one-way street and made a slow, wide turn west into 22nd Street, a two-way street, because a moving van was parked near the corner of 22nd Street. As I completed my turn, a station wagon going east on 22nd Street hit me. The driver of the station wagon said he put on his brakes but he skidded on some oil that was on the street. The driver of the van saw the accident from his cab and told me that the station wagon skidded as he put on his brakes. Patrolman Jack Reed, Badge #24578, who was at the southeast corner of the intersection, saw what happened and made some notes in his memo book.

   Persons Injured – Names and Addresses. If none, state NONE:
   Witnesses – Names and Addresses: If none, state NONE:
      Jack Reed, 33-47 83rd Drive
      Thomas Quinn: 527 Flatlands Avenue

                                 Report prepared by: John Smith
                                 Title: Motor Vehicle Operator

19. According to the report, the accident happened on
    A. Friday, between 6:00 A.M. and 12:00 Noon
    B. Friday, between 12:00 Noon and 6:00 P.M.
    C. Tuesday, between 6:00 A.M. and 12:00 Noon
    D. Monday, between 12:00 Noon and 6:00 P.M.

19._____

20. Which one of the following numbers is part of the driver's license of the operator of the city vehicle?
    A. 3984   B. 5247   C. 4782   D. 7851

20._____

21. The address of the driver of the city vehicle is
    A. not given in the report   B. 427 E. 198th Street
    C. 582 E. 92nd Street   D. 33-47 83rd Drive

21._____

22. A section of the report that is NOT properly filled out is
    A. Witnesses   B. Description of Accident
    C. Persons Injured   D. Damage to Vehicle

22._____

23. According to the accident report, if the only witnesses were the patrolman and the van driver, then the van driver's name is
    A. Reed   B. Quinn   C. Jones   D. Greene

23._____

24. According to the report, the diagram that would BEST show where the cars collided and where the moving van (v) was parked at the time of the accident is

24._____

25. According to the information in the report, it would be MOST correct to say that Michael Greene was
    A. the driver of the station wagon   B. a passenger in the station wagon
    C. the owner of the moving van   D. the owner of the station wagon

25._____

26. According to the information in the report, a factor which contributed to the accident was 26.____
    A. a slippery road condition
    B. bad brakes of one car
    C. obstructed view of traffic light caused by parked van
    D. windshield wipers on the city car not operating properly

27. When a driver makes a report such as this, it is MOST important that he 27.____
    A. print the information so that his supervisor can read it quickly
    B. keep it short because a long report makes it look as though he is hiding a mistake behind many words
    C. show clearly why the accident isn't his fault
    D. give all the facts accurately and completely

28. The first two letters or numbers in the City Vehicle Code Number indicate the type of vehicle. Two letters indicate an 8 passenger 8-cylinder car; two numbers indicates a 6 passenger, 8-cylinder car; a letter followed by a number indicates a 6 passenger 6-cylinder car; a number followed by a letter indicate an 8-cylinder station wagon. 28.____
    The city car involved in this accident is, therefore, a(n)
    A. 8-cylinder station wagon   B. 6 passenger 6-cylinder car
    C. 6 passenger 8-cylinder car   D. 8 passenger 8-cylinder car

29. From the information in the report, the driver of the city vehicle may have been partially at fault because he 29.____
    A. appears to have begun his turn from the wrong lane
    B. appears to have entered the wrong lane of traffic
    C. did not blow his horn as he made the turn
    D. should have braked as he made the turn

30. What evidence is there in the report that the two vehicles collided in front, driver's side? 30.____
    A. The description of the accident
    B. There is no such evidence
    C. The type of damage to the vehicles
    D. The van driver's statement

KEY (CORRECT ANSWERS)

1.	A	11.	B	21.	A
2.	C	12.	B	22.	C
3.	D	13.	A	23.	B
4.	A	14.	B	24.	D
5.	D	15.	D	25.	D
6.	B	16.	A	26.	A
7.	C	17.	B	27.	D
8.	D	18.	A	28.	B
9.	C	19.	C	29.	B
10.	A	20.	A	30.	C

TEST 3

DIRECTIONS: Each question or incomplete statement is followed by several suggested answers or completions. Select the one that BEST answers the question or completes the statement. *PRINT THE LETTER OF THE CORRECT ANSWER IN THE SPACE AT THE RIGHT.*

Questions 1-7.

DIRECTIONS: Questions 1 through 7, inclusive, are to be answered on the basis of the following passage.

DRINKING AND DRIVING

In fatal traffic accidents, a drinking driver is involved more than 30% of the time; on holiday weekends, more than 50% of the fatal accidents involve drinking drivers. Drinking to any extent reduces the judgment, self-control, and driving ability of any driver. Social drinkers, especially those who think they drive better after a drink, are a greater menace than commonly believed, and they outnumber the obviously intoxicated. Two cocktails may reduce visual acuity as much as wearing dark glasses at night. Alcohol is not a stimulant; it is classified medically as a depressant. Coffee or other stimulants will not offset the effects of alcohol; only time can eliminate alcohol from the bloodstream. It takes at least three hours to eliminate one ounce of pure alcohol from the bloodstream.

1. Alcohol is classified by doctors as a
   A. stimulant   B. sedative   C. depressant   D. medicine

2. Social drinkers
   A. never become obviously intoxicated
   B. always drink in large groups
   C. drive better after two cocktails
   D. are a greater menace than commonly believed

3. Alcohol will BEST be eliminated from the bloodstream by
   A. fresh air   B. a stimulant   C. coffee   D. time

4. More than half of the fatal accidents on holiday weekends involve _____ drivers.
   A. inexperienced   B. drinking   C. fast   D. slow

5. Drinking to any extent does NOT
   A. impair judgment
   B. decrease visual acuity
   C. reduce accident potential
   D. affect driving ability

6. In traffic accidents resulting in death, a drinking driver is involved
   A. about one-third of the time
   B. mainly at night
   C. more than 80% of the time
   D. practically all the time on weekends

7. After taking two alcoholic drinks, it is BEST not to drive until you have   7.____
   A. had a cup of black coffee
   B. waited three hours
   C. eaten a full meal
   D. taken a half-hour nap

Questions 8-12.

DIRECTIONS: Questions 8 through 12 are to be answered ONLY on the basis of the information contained in the following accident report.

REPORT OF ACCIDENT

Date of Accident: Nov. 27, ____ Time: 2:20 P.M. Date of Report: 11/28

Department Vehicle	Vehicle No. 2
Operator's Name: John Doe	Operator's Name: Richard Roe
Title: Motor Vehicle Operator	Operator's Address: 983 E. 84th St.
Vehicle Code No.: 17-129	Owner's Name: Robert Roe
License Plate No.: IN-2345	Owner's Address: 983 E. 84th St.
Damage to Vehicle: Crumpled and torn front left fender, broken left headlight, front bumper bent outward on left side, hubcap dented badly and torn off	License Plate No.: 9Y-8765
	Damage to Vehicle: Crumpled right front fender, broken right headlight and parking light, right left front side of front bumper badly bent

Place of Accident: 71st & 3rd Ave.

DESCRIPTION OF ACCIDENT: I was driving west on 71st St. and started to turn north into 3rd Avenue since the light was still green for me. I stopped at the crosswalk because a woman was in the middle of 3rd Avenue crossing from west to east. She had just cleared my car when a Ford sedan, going north, crashed into my left front fender. The light was green on 3rd Ave. when he hit me. The woman who had crossed the avenue in front of me, and whose name I got as a witness, was standing on the corner when I got out of the car.

Persons Injured

_____   _____

_____   _____
Mrs. Mary Brown   Witness   215 E. 71 St.

                                  Report prepared by: John Doe
                                  Title: Motor Vehicle Operator
                                  Badge #17832

3 (#3)

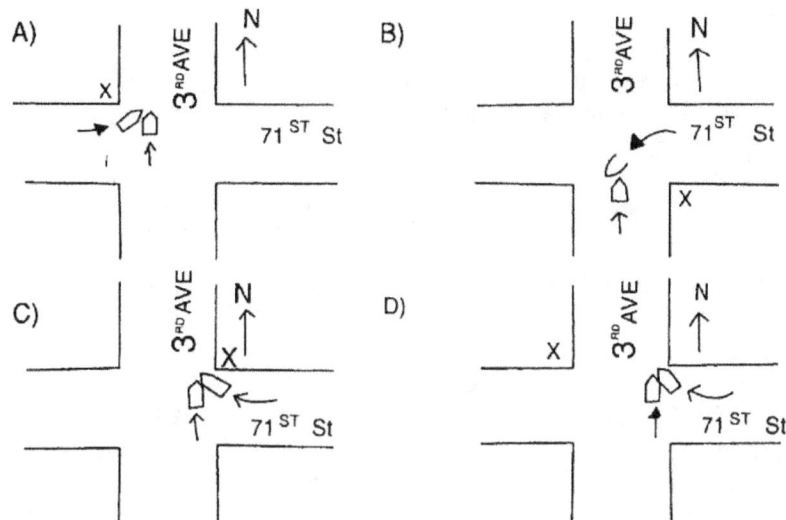

8. According to the description of the accident, the diagram that would BEST show how and where the vehicles crashed and the position of the witness (X) is
   A. A B. B C. C D. D

9. The pedestrian mentioned in the description of the accident was
   A. an unknown woman
   B. Mary Brown
   C. an unknown man
   D. Robert Roe

10. According to the information in the report, the one of the following statements which is INCORRECT is:
    A. Both cars were moving when the accident happened
    B. One car was moving when the accident happened
    C. The Department car was headed northwest when the accident happened
    D. The traffic lights had changed just before the accident happened

11. From the description of the accident as given in the report, the accident would PROBABLY be classified as
    A. premeditated   B. calamitous   C. minor   D. fatal

12. From a reading of the accident report, it can be seen that
    A. the witness was completely unfamiliar with the neighborhood in which the accident took place
    B. the accident occurred in the early hours of the morning
    C. neither driver owned the vehicle he was driving
    D. it was raining when the accident took place

Questions 13-24.

DIRECTIONS: Questions 13 through 24 are based on the description of an automobile accident given below. Read the description carefully before answering these questions.

DESCRIPTION OF AUTOMOBILE ACCIDENT

Ten persons were injured, two critically, when a driverless auto—its accelerator jammed-up ran wild through the busy intersection at 8th Ave. and 42nd Street at 11:30 A.M. yesterday. The car struck a truck, overturned it, and mounted the sidewalk. Several persons were bowled over before the car was finally stopped by collision with a second truck. Police Officer Fred Black, Badge No. 82143, said that the freak accident occurred after the car's driver, Mrs. Mary Jones, 39, of Queens, got out of the car with her daughter, Gloria, aged 3, while the engine was still running. Mr. Herbert Field, 64, of the Bronx, a passenger in the car, accidentally stepped on the accelerator when he tried to get out. This caused the car to shoot forward because the shift was in *drive*, and 5 pedestrians were thrown to the ground.

13. This accident occurred
    A. late in the morning
    B. early in the morning
    C. early in the afternoon
    D. late in the evening

14. The number of persons who were injured, but not critically, is
    A. 2   B. 5   C. 8   D. 10

15. This accident occurred a block away from
    A. Grand Central Terminal
    B. Times Square
    C. Union Square
    D. Pennsylvania Station

16. The runaway car was finally stopped just after it
    A. mounted the sidewalk
    B. collided with a second truck
    C. crossed the intersection
    D. bowled over several persons

17. It can be inferred from the description that the driverless auto had
    A. power brakes
    B. power steering
    C. a turn indicator
    D. an automatic shift

18. The number on the police officer's badge is
    A. 82314   B. 82413   C. 82143   D. 82341

19. The first name of the driver of the car is
    A. Mary   B. Fred   C. Gloria   D. Herbert

20. According to the accident description, the adult passenger lives in
    A. the Bronx, and so does the driver
    B. Queens, and so does the driver
    C. the Bronx, and the driver in Queens
    D. Queens, and the driver in the Bronx

21. The number of pedestrians who were thrown to the ground is 21.____
    A. 2 B. 5 C. 7 D. 10

22. The person who made a statement about the runaway car was 22.____
    A. Herbert Field B. Mary Jones
    C. Gloria Jones D. Fred Black

23. Herbert Field is older than Mary Jones by about _____ years. 23.____
    A. 25 B. 35 C. 51 D. 61

24. The car shot forward immediately after 24.____
    A. Mrs. Jones placed the shift in *drive*
    B. Mr. Field stepped on the accelerator
    C. Mrs. Jones stepped out of the car
    D. Mr. Field got out of the car

Questions 25-28.

DIRECTIONS: Questions 25 through 28 are to be answered ONLY on the basis of the information given in the following passage.

ACCIDENT PRONESS

Accident proneness is a subject deserving much more attention than it has received. Studies have shown a high incidence of accidents to be associated with particular employees who are called accident prone. Such employees, according to these studies, behave on their jobs in ways which make them likely to have more accidents than would normally be expected.

It is important to point out the difference between the employee who is a *repeater* and the one who is truly accident prone. It is obvious that any person assigned to work about which he knows little will be liable to injury until he does learn the *how* of the job. Few workers left completely on their own will develop adequate safe practices. Therefore, they must be trained. Only those who fail to respond to proper training should be regarded as accident prone.

The dangers of an occupation should also be considered when judging an accident record. For a crane operator, a record of five accidents in a given period of time may not indicate accident proneness, while, in the case of a clerk, two accidents over the same period of time may be excessive. There are the reporters whose accident records can be explained by correctible physical defects, by correctible unsafe plant or machine conditions, or by assignment to work for which they are not suited because they cannot meet all the job's physical requirements. Such repeaters cannot be fairly called *accident prone*. A diagnosis of accident proneness should not be lightly made but should be based on all of these considerations.

25. According to the above passage, studies have shown that accident prone 25.____
    employees
    A. work under unsafe physical conditions
    B. act in unsafe ways on the job
    C. are not usually physically suited for their jobs
    D. work in the more dangerous occupations

26. According to the above passage, a person who is accident prone   26.____
    A. has received proper training which has not reduced his tendency toward accidents
    B. repeats the same accident several times over a short period of time
    C. experiences excessive anxiety about dangers in his occupation
    D. ignores unsafe but correctible machine conditions

27. According to the above passage, MOST persons who are given work they   27.____
    know little about
    A. will eventually learn on their own sufficient safety practices to follow
    B. work safely if they are not accident prone
    C. must be trained before they develop adequate safety methods
    D. should be regarded as accident prone until they become familiar with the job

28. According to the above passage, to effectively judge the accident record of an   28.____
    employee, one should consider
    A. the employee's age and physical condition
    B. that five accidents are excessive
    C. the type of dangers that are natural to his job
    D. the difficulty level of previous occupations held by the employee

Questions 29-30.

DIRECTIONS: Questions 29 and 30 are to be answered ONLY on the basis of the information given in the following passage.

When heavy rain beats on your windshield, it becomes hard for you to see ahead and even harder to see objects to the side—despite good windshield wipers. Also, the danger zone becomes longer when it is raining because the car takes longer to stop on wet streets. Remember that the danger zone of your car is the distance within which you can't stop after you have seen something on the road ahead of your car. The way to reduce the length of the danger zone of your car while driving is to reduce speed.

29. From the information in the above passage, you cannot tell if the danger zone   29.____
    of your car
    A. can be made smaller
    B. is greater on a rainy day
    C. is greater on cloudy days than on clear days
    D. is the distance in back of the car or in front of the car

30. According to the above passage, the danger zone of a moving car is affected   30.____
    by
    A. the condition of the street and the speed of the car
    B. many things which cannot be pinned down, in addition to the mechanical condition of the car
    C. the number of objects to the front and to the side
    D. visibility of the road and the reaction time of the driver

KEY (CORRECT ANSWERS)

1.	C	11.	C	21.	B
2.	D	12.	C	22.	D
3.	D	13.	A	23.	A
4.	B	14.	C	24.	B
5.	C	15.	B	25.	B
6.	A	16.	B	26.	A
7.	B	17.	D	27.	C
8.	C	18.	C	28.	C
9.	B	19.	A	29.	C
10.	A	20.	C	30.	A

EXAMINATION SECTION
TEST 1

DIRECTIONS: Each question or incomplete statement is followed by several suggested answers or completions. Select the one that BEST answers the question or completes the statement. *PRINT THE LETTER OF THE CORRECT ANSWER IN THE SPACE AT THE RIGHT.*

1. Which of the following sentences is punctuated INCORRECTLY?   1.____
   A. Johnson said, "One tiny virus, Blanche, can multiply so fast that it will become 200 viruses in 25 minutes."
   B. With economic pressures hitting them from all sides, American farmers have become the weak link in the food chain.
   C. The degree to which this is true, of course, depends on the personalities of the people involved, the subject matter, and the atmosphere in general.
   D. "What loneliness, asked George Eliot, is more lonely than distrust?"

2. Which of the following sentences is punctuated INCORRECTLY?   2.____
   A. Based on past experiences, do you expect the plumber to show up late, not have the right parts, and overcharge you.
   B. When polled, however, the participants were most concerned that it be convenient.
   C. No one mentioned the flavor of the coffee, and no one seemed to care that china was used instead of plastic.
   D. As we said before, sometimes people view others as things; they don't see them as living, breathing beings like themselves.

3. Convention members travelled here from Kingston New York Pittsfield   3.____
   Massachusetts Bennington Vermont and Hartford Connecticut.
   How many commas should there be in the above sentence?
   A. 3   B. 4   C. 5   D. 6

4. Of the two speakers the one who spoke about human rights is more famous   4.____
   and more humble.
   How many commas should there be in the above sentence?
   A. 1   B. 2   C. 3   D. 4

5. Which sentence is punctuated INCORRECTLY?   5.____
   A. Five people voted no; two voted yes; one person abstained.
   B. Well, consider what has been said here today, but we won't make any promises.
   C. Anthropologists divide history into three major periods: the Stone Age, the Bronze Age, and the Iron Age.
   D. Therefore, we may create a stereotype about people who are unsuccessful; we may see them as lazy, unintelligent, or afraid of success.

6. Which sentence is punctuated INCORRECTLY? 6.____
    A. Studies have found that the unpredictability of customer behavior can lead to a great deal of stress, particularly if the behavior is unpleasant or if the employee has little control over it.
    B. If this degree of emotion and variation can occur in spectator sports, imagine the role that perceptions can play when there are <u>real</u> stakes involved.
    C. At other times, however hidden expectations may sabotage or severely damage an encounter without anyone knowing what happened.
    D. There are usually four issues to look for in a conflict: differences in values, goals, methods, and facts.

Questions 7-10.

DIRECTIONS: Questions 7 through 10 test your ability to distinguish between words that sound alike but are spelled differently and have different meanings. In the following groups of sentences, one of the underlined words is used incorrectly.

7. A. By <u>accepting</u> responsibility for their actions, managers promote trust. 7.____
    B. Dropping hints or making <u>illusions</u> to things that you would like changed sometimes leads to resentment.
    C. The entire unit <u>loses</u> respect for the manager and resents the reprimand.
    D. Many people are <u>averse</u> to confronting problems directly; they would rather avoid them.

8. A. What does this say about the <u>effect</u> our expectations have on those we supervise? 8.____
    B. In an effort to save time between 9 A.M. and 1 P.M., the staff members devised <u>their</u> own interpretation of what was to be done on these forms.
    C. The taskmaster's <u>principal</u> concern is for getting the work done; he or she is not concerned about the need or interests of employees.
    D. The advisor's main objective was increasing Angela's ability to invest her <u>capitol</u> wisely.

9. A. A typical problem is that people have to cope with the internal <u>censer</u> of their feelings. 9.____
    B. Sometimes, in their attempt to sound more learned, people speak in ways that are barely <u>comprehensible</u>.
    C. The <u>council</u> will meet next Friday to decide whether Abrams should continue as representative.
    D. His <u>descent</u> from grace was assured by that final word.

10. A. The doctor said that John's leg had to remain <u>stationary</u> or it would not heal properly. 10.____
    B. There is a city <u>ordinance</u> against parking too close to fire hydrants.
    C. Meyer's problem is that he is never <u>discrete</u> when talking about office politics.
    D. Mrs. Thatcher probably worked harder <u>than</u> any other British Prime Minister had ever worked.

Questions 11-20.

DIRECTIONS: For each of the following groups of sentences in Questions 11 through 20, select the sentence which is the BEST example of English usage and grammar.

11. A. She is a woman who, at age sixty, is distinctly attractive and cares about how they look.
    B. It was a seemingly impossible search, and no one knew the problems better than she.
    C. On the surface, they are all sweetness and light, but his morbid character is under it.
    D. The minicopier, designed to appeal to those who do business on the run like architects in the field or business travelers, weigh about four pounds.

11.____

12. A. Neither the administrators nor the union representative regret the decision to settle the disagreement.
    B. The plans which are made earlier this year were no longer being considered.
    C. I would have rode with him if I had known he was leaving at five.
    D. I don't know who she said had it.

12.____

13. A. Writing at a desk, the memo was handed to her for immediate attention.
    B. Carla didn't water Carl's plants this week, which she never does.
    C. Not only are they good workers, with excellent writing and speaking skills, and they get to the crux of any problem we hand them.
    D. We've noticed that this enthusiasm for undertaking new projects sometimes interferes with his attention to detail.

13.____

14. A. It's obvious that Nick offends people by being unruly, inattentive, and having no patience.
    B. Marcia told Genie that she would have to leave soon.
    C. Here are the papers you need to complete your investigation.
    D. Julio was startled by you're comment.

14.____

15. A. The new manager has done good since receiving her promotion, but her secretary has helped her a great deal.
    B. One of the personnel managers approached John and tells him that the client arrived unexpectedly.
    C. If somebody can supply us with the correct figures, they should do so immediately.
    D. Like zealots, advocates seek power because they want to influence the policies and actions of an organization.

15.____

16. A. Between you and me, Chris probably won't finish this assignment in time.
    B. Rounding the corner, the snack bar appeared before us.
    C. Parker's radical reputation made to the Supreme Court his appointment impossible.
    D. By the time we arrived, Marion finishes briefing James and returns to Hank's office.

16.____

17. A. As we pointed out earlier, the critical determinant of the success of middle managers is their ability to communicate well with others.
    B. The lecturer stated there wasn't no reason for bad supervision.
    C. We are well aware whose at fault in this instance.
    D. When planning important changes, it's often wise to seek the participation of others because employees often have much valuable ideas to offer.

17.____

18. A. Joan had ought to throw out those old things that were damaged when the roof leaked.
    B. I spose he'll let us know what he's decided when he finally comes to a decision.
    C. Carmen was walking to work when she suddenly realized that she had left her lunch on the table as she passed the market.
    D. Are these enough plants for your new office?

18.____

19. A. First move the lever forward, and then they should lift the ribbon casing before trying to take it out.
    B. Michael finished quickest than any other person in the office.
    C. There is a special meeting for we committee members today at 4 p.m.
    D. My husband is worried about our having to work overtime next week.

19.____

20. A. Another source of conflicts are individuals who possess very poor interpersonal skills.
    B. It is difficult for us to work with him on projects because these kinds of people are not interested in team building.
    C. Each of the departments was represented at the meeting.
    D. Poor boy, he never should of past that truck on the right.

20.____

Questions 21-28.

DIRECTIONS: In Questions 21 through 28, there may be a problem with English grammar or usage. If a problem does exist, select the letter that indicates the most effective change. If no problem exists, select Choice A.

21. He rushed her to the hospital and stayed with her, even though this took quite a bit of his time, he didn't charge her anything.
    A. No changes are necessary.
    B. Change even though to although
    C. Change the first comma to a period and capitalize even
    D. Change rushed to had rushed

21.____

22. Waiting that appears unfairly feels longer than waiting that seems justified. 22.____
    A. No changes are necessary. B. Change unfairly to unfair
    C. Change appears to seems D. Change longer to longest

23. May be you and the person who argued with you will be able to reach an 23.____
    agreement.
    A. No changes are necessary
    B. Change will be to were
    C. Change argued with to had an argument with
    D. Change May be to Maybe

24. Any one of them could of taken the file while you were having coffee. 24.____
    A. No changes are necessary
    B. Change any one to anyone
    C. Change of to have
    D. Change were having to were out having

25. While people get jobs or move from poverty level to better paying employment, 25.____
    they stop receiving benefits and start paying taxes.
    A. No changes are necessary B. Change While to As
    C. Change stop to will stop D. Change get to obtain

26. Maribeth's phone rang while talking to George about the possibility of their 26.____
    meeting Tom at three this afternoon.
    A. No changes are necessary
    B. Change their to her
    C. Move to George so that it follows Tom
    D. Change talking to she was talking

27. According to their father, Lisa is smarter than Chris, but Emily is the smartest 27.____
    of the three sisters.
    A. No changes are necessary
    B. Change their to her
    C. Change is to was
    D. Make two sentences, changing the second comma to a period and
       omitting but

28. Yesterday, Mark and he claim that Carl took Carol's ideas and used them 28.____
    inappropriately.
    A. No changes are necessary
    B. Change claim to claimed
    C. Change inappropriately to inappropriate
    D. Change Carol's to Carols'

Questions 29-34.

DIRECTIONS: For each group of sentences in Questions 29 through 34, select the choice that represents the BEST editing of the problem sentence.

29. The managers expected employees to be at their desks at all times, but they would always be late or leave unannounced.
    A. The managers wanted employees to always be at their desks, but they would always be late or leave unannounced.
    B. Although the managers expected employees to be at their desks no matter what came up, they would always be late and leave without telling anyone.
    C. Although the managers expected employees to be at their desks at all times, the managers would always be late or leave without telling anyone.
    D. The managers expected the employee to never leave their desks, but they would always be late or leave without telling anyone.

29.____

30. The one who is department manager he will call you to discuss the problem tomorrow morning at 10 A.M.
    A. The one who is department manager will call you tomorrow morning at ten to discuss the problem.
    B. The department manager will call you to discuss the problem tomorrow at 10 A.M.
    C. Tomorrow morning at 10 A.M., the department manager will call you to discuss the problem.
    D. Tomorrow morning the department manager will call you to discuss the problem.

30.____

31. A conference on child care in the workplace the $200 cost of which to attend may be prohibitive to childcare workers who earn less than that weekly.
    A. A conference on child care in the workplace that costs $200 may be too expensive for childcare workers who earn less than that each week.
    B. A conference on child care in the workplace, the cost of which to attend is $200, may be prohibitive to childcare workers who earn less than that weekly.
    C. A conference on child care in the workplace who costs $200 may be too expensive for childcare workers who earn less than that a week.
    D. A conference on child care in the workplace which costs $200 may be too expensive to childcare workers who earn less than that on a weekly basis.

31.____

32. In accordance with estimates recently made, there are 40,000 to 50,000 nuclear weapons in our world today.
    A. Because of estimates recently, there are 40,000 to 50,000 nuclear weapons in the world today.
    B. In accordance with estimates made recently, there are 40,000 to 50,000 nuclear weapons in the world today.

32.____

C. According to estimates made recently, there are 40,000 to 50,000 weapons in the world today.
D. According to recent estimates, there are 40,000 to 50,000 nuclear weapons in the world today.

33. Motivation is important in problem solving, but they say that excessive motivation can inhibit the creative process.
    A. Motivation is important in problem solving, but, as they say, too much of it can inhibit the creative process.
    B. Motivation is important in problem solving and excessive motivation will inhibit the creative process.
    C. Motivation is important in problem solving, but excessive motivation can inhibit the creative process.
    D. Motivation is important in problem solving because excessive motivation can inhibit the creative process.

33._____

34. In selecting the best option calls for consulting with all the people that are involved in it.
    A. In selecting the best option consulting with all people concerned with it.
    B. Calling for the best option, we consulted all the affected people.
    C. We called all the people involved to select the best option.
    D. To be sure of selecting the best option, one should consult all the people involved.

34._____

35. There are a number of problems with the following letter. From the options below, select the version that is MOST in accordance with standard business style, tone, and form.

35._____

Dear Sir:

   We are so sorry that we have had to backorder your order for 15,000 widgets and 2,300 whatzits for such a long time. We have been having incredibly bad luck lately. When your order first came in no one could get to it because my secretary was out with the flu and her replacement didn't know what she was doing, then there was the dock strike in Cucamonga which held things up for awhile, and then it just somehow got lost. We think it may have fallen behind the radiator.
   We are happy to say that all these problems have been taken care of, we are caught up on supplies, and we should have the stuff to you soon, in the near future—about two weeks. You may not believe us after everything you've been through with us, but it's true.
   We'll let you know as soon as we have a secure date for delivery. Thank you so much for continuing to do business with us after all the problems this probably has caused you.

Yours very sincerely,
Rob Barker

8 (#1)

A. Dear Sir:

   We are so sorry that we have had to backorder your order for 15,000 widgets and 2,300 whatzits. We have been having problems with staff lately and the dock strike hasn't helped anything.
   We are happy to say that all these problems have been taken care of. I've told my secretary to get right on it, and we should have the stuff to you soon. Thank you so much for continuing to do business with us after all the problems this must have caused you.
   We'll let you know as soon as we have a secure date for delivery.

   Sincerely,
   Rob Barker

B. Dear Sir:

   We regret that we haven't been able to fill your order for 15,000 widgets and 2,300 whatzits in a timely fashion.
   We'll let you know as soon as we have a secure date for delivery.

   Sincerely,
   Rob Barker

C. Dear Sir:

   We are so very sorry that we haven't been able to fill your order for 15,000 widgets and 2,300 whatzits. We have been having incredibly bad luck lately, but things are much better now.
   Thank you so much for bearing with us through all of this. We'll let you know as soon as we have a secure date for delivery.

   Sincerely,
   Rob Barker

D. Dear Sir:

   We are very sorry that we haven't been able to fill your order for 15,000 widgets and 2,300 whatzits. Due to unforeseen difficulties, we have had to back-order your request. At this time, supplies have caught up to demand, and we foresee a delivery date within the next two weeks.
   We'll let you know as soon as we have a secure date for delivery. Thank you for your patience.

   Sincerely,
   Rob Barker

KEY (CORRECT ANSWERS)

1.	D	11.	B	21.	C	31.	A
2.	A	12.	D	22.	B	32.	D
3.	B	13.	D	23.	D	33.	C
4.	A	14.	C	24.	C	34.	D
5.	B	15.	D	25.	B	35.	D
6.	C	16.	A	26.	D		
7.	B	17.	A	27.	A		
8.	D	18.	D	28.	B		
9.	A	19.	D	29.	C		
10.	C	20.	C	30.	B		

EXAMINATION SECTION
TEST 1

DIRECTIONS: Each question or incomplete statement is followed by several suggested answers or completions. Select the one that *BEST* answers the question or completes the statement. *PRINT THE LETTER OF THE CORRECT ANSWER IN THE SPACE AT THE RIGHT.*

READING COMPREHENSION.

Questions 1-4. Read the passage below and answer the following questions by selecting the best of the five suggested answers.

Visitors will arrive at the north gate in six 17-passenger buses. An automobile from the installation will bring three visiting officials to this gate. The automobile will arrive at 2:00 p.m. Two of the buses will arrive there at 2:20 p.m. and the others at 2:40 p.m. The vehicles will move from the gate south along Hamilton Street to Main Avenue. They will proceed east on Main, and discharge the passengers at the foot of the steps at the front of the Headquarters Building. Four of the buses and the automobile will wait to load those visitors who are going to the southwest area. Two of the buses will rejoin the shuttle bus service for the installation.

1. The gate to which the visitors are to come is the

    A. north
    B. south
    C. east
    D. west
    E. southeast

1.____

2. The number of buses to be used to bring visitors to the gate specified is

    A. 2
    B. 6
    C. 7
    D. 10
    E. 17

2.____

3. The number of vehicles that will wait at the Headquarters Building to carry visitors and visiting officials to the southwest area is

    A. 1
    B. 2
    C. 4
    D. 5
    E. 6

3.____

4. The visiting officials will be riding in_____.

    A. the leading bus
    B. an automobile
    C. a bus arriving at 2:20 p.m.
    D. the last bus to arrive
    E. several buses

4.____

Question 5-6. Answer the question below based on the following passages.

What constitutes skill in any line of work is not always easy to determine; economy of time must be carefully distinguished from economy of energy, as the quickest method may require the greatest expenditure of muscular effort, and may not be essential or at all desirable.

5. *The passage best supports the statement that*

    A. energy and time cannot both be conserved in the performing of a single task
    B. the most efficiently executed task is not always the one done in the shortest time
    C. if a task requires muscular energy, it is not being performed economically
    D. skill in performing a task should not be acquired at the expense of time
    E. a task is well done when it is performed in the shortest time

In the business districts of cities, collections from street letter boxes are made at stated hours, and collectors are required to observe these hours exactly. Any businessman using these boxes can rely with certainty upon the time of the next collection.

6. *The passage best supports the statement that* an important characteristic of mail collections is their

    A. cheapness
    B. extent
    C. safety
    D. speed
    E. regularity

VERBAL ABILITIES.

Questions 7-8. For each question, choose the one of the five suggested answers that means the most nearly the same as the word in *italics*.

7. A small crane was used to *raise* the heavy parts.
   Raise means most nearly

    A. drag
    B. unload
    C. deliver
    D. lift
    E. guide

8. The reports were *consolidated* by the secretary. *Consolidated* means most nearly

    A. combined
    B. concluded
    C. distributed
    D. protected
    E. weighed

Questions 9-11. For each question, select the word or group of words lettered A, B, C, D, or E that means most nearly the same as the word in capital letters.

9. PREVIOUS means most nearly

    A. abandoned
    B. former
    C. timely
    D. successive
    E. younger

10. To ENCOUNTER means most nearly to

    A. recall
    B. overcome
    C. weaken
    D. retreat
    E. meet

11. A FUNDAMENTAL point is one that is

    A. difficult
    B. drastic
    C. essential
    D. emphasized
    E. final

NUMBER AND NAME COMPARISONS

Questions 12-14. In each line across the page there are three names or numbers that are much alike. Compare the three names or numbers and decide which ones are exactly alike. Choose the letter:
  A) if ALL THREE names or numbers are exactly ALIKE
  B) if only the FIRST and SECOND names or numbers are exactly ALIKE
  C) if only the FIRST and THIRD names or numbers are exactly ALIKE
  D) if only the SECOND and THIRD names or numbers are exactly ALIKE
  E) if ALL THREE names or numbers are DIFFERENT

12.   June Allan   Jane Allan   Jane Allan

13.   10235   10235   10235

14.   32614   32164   32614

Questions 15-52. Each of the boxes below is labeled A, B, C, D, or E and contains the names of several people. Each question following is a name. For each question, choose the letter A, B, C, D, or E, depending upon which of these boxes the name is in.

A	B	C	D	E
Redman Payne Carter Conlow	Denton Rayburn Sanford Eastlake	Teller Moore Garvey Randall	Edison Miller Appleton Loman	Wheeler Forest Simmons Camp

4 (#1)

15. Loman 15.____
16. Edison 16.____
17. Eastlake 17.____
18. Garvey 18.____
19. Payne 19.____
20. Miller 20.____
21. Redman 21.____
22. Carter 22.____
23. Denton 23.____
24. Sanford 24.____
25. Denton 25.____
26. Payne 26.____
27. Simmons 27.____
28. Edison 28.____
29. Conlow 29.____
30. Randall 30.____
31. Conlow 31.____
32. Rayburn 32.____
33. Eastlake 33.____
34. Appleton 34.____
35. Teller 35.____
36. Simmons 36.____
37. Payne 37.____
38. Camp 38.____
39. Miller 39.____
40. Garvey 40.____
41. Randall 41.____
42. Wheeler 42.____
43. Redman 43.____

5 (#1)

44. Moore 44.____
45. Appleton 45.____
46. Forest 46.____
47. Moore 47.____
48. Teller 48.____
49. Carter 49.____
50. Wheeler 50.____
51. Edison 51.____
52. Rayburn 52.____

Questions 53-70. You will be given addresses to compare. Choose the letter A if the two addresses are exactly *Alike* in every way. Choose the letter D if they are *Different*.

#			
53.	2134 S 20th St	2134 S 20th St	53.____
54.	4608 N Warnock St	4806 N Warnock St	54.____
55.	1202 W Girard Dr	1202 WGirard Rd	55.____
56.	3120 S Harcourt St	3120 S Harcourt St	56.____
57.	4618 WAddison St	4618 E Addison St	57.____
58.	39-B Parkway Rd	39-D Parkway Rd	58.____
59.	6425 N Delancey	6425 N Delancey	59.____
60.	5407 Columbia Rd	5407 Columbia Rd	60.____
61.	2106 Southern Ave	2106 Southern Ave	61.____
62.	HightailsN C	Highlands N C	62.____
63.	2873 Pershing Dr	2873 Pershing Dr	63.____
64.	1329 N H Ave NW	1329 N J Ave NW	64.____
65.	1316 N Quinn St Arl	1316 N Quinn St Alex	65.____
66.	7507 Wyngate Dr	7505 Wyngate Dr	66.____
67.	2918 Colesville Rd	2918 Colesville Rd	67.____
68.	2071 Belvedere Dr	2071 Belvedere Dr	68.____
69.	Palmer Wash	Palmer Mich	69.____
70.	2106 16th St SW	2106 16th St SW	70.____

69

MATHEMATICAL ABILITY

Questions 71-75. Solve each problem and see which of the suggested answers A, B, C, or D is correct. If your answer does not exactly agree with any of the four suggested answers, choose letter E.

71. Add:

    963
    257
    416

    A. 1,516   B. 1,526   C. 1,636   D. 1,726
    E. none of these

72. Subtract:

    33
    8

    A. 25   B. 26   C. 35   D. 36
    E. none of these

73. Multiply:

    45
    5

    A. 200   B. 215   C. 225   D. 235
    E. none of these

74. Divide:

    $40\sqrt{1,208}$

    A. 3   B. 30   C. 33   D. 40
    E. none of these

75. If 2 men can distribute 7,000 letters in 2 hours, in how many hours would they distribute 17,500 letters, at the same rate?

    A. 3 hours   B. 4 1/2 hours   C. 5 hours   D. 10 hours
    E. none of these

KEY (CORRECT ANSWERS)

1. A	16. D	31. A	46. E	61. A
2. B	17. B	32. B	47. C	62. D
3. D	18. C	33. B	48. C	63. A
4. B	19. A	34. D	49. A	64. D
5. B	20. D	35. C	50. E	65. D
6. E	21. A	36. E	51. D	66. D
7. D	22. A	37. A	52. B	67. A
8. A	23. B	38. E	53. A	68. A
9. B	24. B	39. D	54. D	69. D
10. E	25. B	40. C	55. D	70. A
11. C	26. A	41. C	56. A	71. C
12. D	27. E	42. E	57. D	72. A
13. A	28. D	43. A	58. D	73. C
14. C	29. A	44. C	59. A	74. E
15. D	30. C	45. D	60. A	75. C

SPELLING

COMMENTARY

Spelling forms an integral part of tests of academic aptitude and achievement and of general and mental ability. Moreover, the spelling question is a staple of verbal and clerical tests in civil service entrance and promotional examinations.

Perhaps, the most rewarding way to learn to spell successfully is the direct, functional approach of learning to spell correctly, both orally and in writing, all words as they appear, both singly and in context.

In accordance with this positive method, the spelling question is presented here in "test" form, as it might appear on an actual examination.

The spelling question may appear on examinations in the following format:
> Four words are listed in each question. These are lettered A, B, C, and D. A fifth option, E, is also given, which always reads "none misspelled." The examinee is to select one of the five (lettered) choices: either A, B, C, or D if one of the words is misspelled, or item E, none misspelled, if all four words have been correctly spelled in the question.

SAMPLE QUESTIONS

The directions for this part are approximately as follows:

DIRECTIONS: Mark the space corresponding to the one MISSPELLED word in each of the following groups of words. If NO word is misspelled, mark the last space on the answer sheet.

SAMPLE O
- A. walk
- B. talk
- C. play
- D. dance
- E. *none misspelled*

Since none of the words is misspelled, E would be marked on the answer sheet.

SAMPLE OO
- A. seize
- B. yield
- C. define
- D. reccless
- E. *none misspelled*

Since "reccless" (correct spelling, reckless) has been misspelled, D would be marked on the answer sheet

CLERICAL ABILITIES
EXAMINATION SECTION
TEST 1

DIRECTIONS: Each question or incomplete statement is followed by several suggested answers or completions. Select the one that BEST answers the question or completes the statement. *PRINT THE LETTER OF THE CORRECT ANSWER IN THE SPACE AT THE RIGHT.*

Questions 1-4.

DIRECTIONS: Questions 1 through 4 are to be answered on the basis of the information given below.

The most commonly used filing system and the one that is easiest to learn is alphabetical filing. This involves putting records in an A to Z order, according to the letters of the alphabet. The name of a person is filed by using the following order: first, the surname or last name; second, the first name; third, the middle name or middle initial. For example, *Henry C. Young* is filed under *Y* and thereafter under *Young, Henry C*. The name of a company is filed in the same way. For example, *Long Cabinet Co.* is filed under *L* while *John T. Long Cabinet Co.* is filed under *L* and thereafter under *Long, John T. Cabinet Co.*

1. The one of the following which lists the names of persons in the CORRECT alphabetical order is: 1.____
   A. Mary Carrie, Helen Carrol, James Carson, John Carter
   B. James Carson, Mary Carrie, John Carter, Helen Carrol
   C. Helen Carrol, James Carson, John Carter, Mary Carrie
   D. John Carter, Helen Carrol, Mary Carrie, James Carson

2. The one of the following which lists the names of persons in the CORRECT alphabetical order is: 2.____
   A. Jones, John C.; Jones, John A.; Jones, John P.; Jones, John K.
   B. Jones, John P.; Jones, John K.; Jones, John C.; Jones, John A.
   C. Jones, John A.; Jones, John C.; Jones, John K.; Jones, John P.
   D. Jones, John K.; Jones, John C.; Jones, John A.; Jones, John P.

3. The one of the following which lists the names of the companies in the CORRECT alphabetical order is: 3.____
   A. Blane Co., Blake Co., Block Co., Blear Co.
   B. Blake Co., Blane Co., Blear Co., Block Co.
   C. Block Co., Blear Co., Blane Co., Blake Co.
   D. Blear Co., Blake Co., Blane Co., Block Co.

4. You are to return to the file an index card on *Barry C. Wayne Materials and Supplies Co.*
Of the following, the CORRECT alphabetical group that you should return the index card to is

A. A to G   B. H to M   C. N to S   D. T to Z

4.____

Questions 5-10.

DIRECTIONS: In each of Questions 5 through 10, the names of four people are given. For each question, choose as your answer the one of the four names given which should be filed FIRST according to the usual system of alphabetical filing of names, as described in the following paragraph.

In filing names, you must start with the last name. Names are filed in order of the first letter of the last name, then the second letter, etc. Therefore, BAILY would be filed before BROWN, which would be filed before COLT. A name with fewer letters of the same type comes first, i.e., Smith before Smithe. If the last names are the same, the names are filed alphabetically by the first name. If the first name is an initial, a name with an initial would come before a first name that starts with the same letter as the initial. Therefore, I. BROWN would come before IRA BROWN. Finally, if both last name and first name are the same, the name would be filed alphabetically by the middle name, once again an initial coming before a middle name which starts with the same letter as the initial. If there is no middle name at all, the name would come before those with middle initials or names.

SAMPLE QUESTION:
    A. Lester Daniels
    B. William Dancer
    C. Nathan Danzig
    D. Dan Lester

The last names beginning with D are filed before the last name beginning with L. Since DANIELS, DANCER, and DANZIG all begin with the same three letters, you must look at the fourth letter of the last name to determine which name should be filed first. C comes before I or Z in the alphabet, so DANCER is filed before DANIELS or DANZIG. Therefore, the answer to the above sample question is B.

5.   A. Scott Biala
        B. Mary Byala
        C. Martin Baylor
        D. Francis Bauer

5.____

6.   A. Howard J. Black
        B. Howard Black
        C. J. Howard Black
        D. John H. Black

6.____

7.   A. Theodora Garth Kingston
        B. Theadore Barth Kingston
        C. Thomas Kingston
        D. Thomas T. Kingston

7.____

8. A. Paulette Mary Huerta
    B. Paul M. Huerta
    C. Paulette L. Huerta
    D. Peter A. Huerta

9. A. Martha Hunt Morgan
    B. Martin Hunt Morgan
    C. Mary H. Morgan
    D. Martine H. Morgan

10. A. James T. Meerschaum
    B. James M. Mershum
    C. James F. Mearshaum
    D. James N. Meshum

Questions 11-14.

DIRECTIONS: Questions 11 through 14 are to be answered SOLELY on the basis of the following information.

You are required to file various documents in file drawers which are labeled according to the following pattern:

DOCUMENTS

MEMOS		LETTERS	
File	Subject	File	Subject
84PM1	(A-L)	84PC1	(A-L)
84PM2	(M-Z)	84PC2	(M-Z)

REPORTS		INQUIRIES	
File	Subject	File	Subject
84PR1	(A-L)	84PQ1	(A-L)
84PR2	(M-Z)	84PQ2	(M-Z)

11. A letter dealing with a burglary should be filed in the drawer labeled
    A. 84PM1   B. 84PC1   C. 84PR1   D. 84PQ2

12. A report on Statistics should be found in the drawer labeled
    A. 84PM1   B. 84PC2   C. 84PR2   D. 84PQS

13. An inquiry is received about parade permit procedures. It should be filed in the drawer labeled
    A. 84PM2   B. 84PC1   C. 84PR1   D. 84PQ2

14. A police officer has a question about a robbery report you filed. You should pull this file from the drawer labeled
    A. 84PM1   B. 84PM2   C. 84PR1   D. 84PR2

Questions 15-22.

DIRECTIONS: Each of Questions 15 through 22 consists of four or six numbered names. For each question, choose the option (A, B, C, or D) which indicates the order in which the names should be filed in accordance with the following filing instructions:
- File alphabetically according to last name, then first name, then middle initial.
- File according to each successive letter within a name.
- When comparing two names in which the letters in the longer name are identical to the corresponding letters in the shorter name, the shorter name is filed first.
- When the last names are the same, initials are always filed before names beginning with the same letter.

15.   I.   Ralph Robinson
      II. Alfred Ross
      III. Luis Robles
      IV. James Roberts

   The CORRECT filing sequence for the above names should be
   A. IV, II, I, III   B. I, IV, III, II   C. III, IV, I, II   D. IV, I, III, II

16.   I.   Irwin Goodwin
      II. Inez Gonzalez
      III. Irene Goodman
      IV. Ira S. Goodwin
      V.   Ruth I. Goldstein
      VI. M.B. Goodman

   The CORRECT filing sequence for the above names should be
   A. V, II, I, IV, III, VI   B. V, II, VI, III, IV, I
   C. V, II, III, VI, IV, I   D. V, II, III, VI, I, IV

17.   I.   George Allan
      II. Gregory Allen
      III. Gary Allen
      IV. George Allen

   The CORRECT filing sequence for the above names should be
   A. IV, III, I, II   B. I, IV, II, III   C. III, IV, I, II   D. I, III, IV, II

18. I. Simon Kauffman
    II. Leo Kaufman
    III. Robert Kaufmann
    IV. Paul Kauffmann

    The CORRECT filing sequence for the above names should be
    A. I, IV, II, III   B. II, IV, III, I   C. III, II, IV, I   D. I, II, III, IV

    18.____

19. I. Roberta Williams
    II. Robin Wilson
    III. Roberta Wilson
    IV. Robin Williams

    The CORRECT filing sequence for the above names should be
    A. III, II, IV, I   B. I, IV, III, II   C. I, II, III, IV   D. III, I, II, IV

    19.____

20. I. Lawrence Shultz
    II. Albert Schultz
    III. Theodore Schwartz
    IV. Thomas Schwarz
    V. Alvin Schultz
    VI. Leonard Shultz

    The CORRECT filing sequence for the above names should be
    A. II, V, III, IV, I, VI   B. IV, III, V, I, II, VI
    C. II, V, I, VI, III, IV   D. I, VI, II, V, III, IV

    20.____

21. I. McArdle
    II. Mayer
    III. Maletz
    IV. McNiff
    V. Meyer
    VI. MacMahon

    The CORRECT filing sequence for the above names should be
    A. I, IV, VI, III, II, V   B. II, I, IV, VI, III, V
    C. VI, III, II, I, IV, V   D. VI, III, II, V, I, IV

    21.____

22. I. Jack E. Johnson
    II. R.H. Jackson
    III. Bertha Jackson
    IV. J.T. Johnson
    V. Ann Johns
    VI. John Jacobs

    The CORRECT filing sequence for the above names should be
    A. II, III, VI, V, IV, I   B. III, II, VI, V, IV, I
    C. VI, II, III, I, V, IV   D. III, II, VI, IV, V, I

    22.____

Questions 23-30.

DIRECTIONS: The code table below shows 10 letters with matching numbers. For each question, there are three sets of letters. Each set of letters is followed by a set of numbers which may or may not match their correct letter according to the code table. For each question, check all three sets of letters and numbers and mark your answer:
  A. if no pairs are correctly matched
  B. if only one pair is correctly matched
  C. if only two pairs are correctly matched
  D. if all three pairs are correctly matched

CODE TABLE

T	M	V	D	S	P	R	G	B	H
1	2	3	4	5	6	7	8	9	0

SAMPLE QUESTION: TMVDSP – 123456
RGBHTM – 789011
DSPRGB – 256789

In the sample question above, the first set of numbers correctly match its set of letters. But the second and third pairs contain mistakes. In the second pair, M is correctly matched with number 1. According to the code table, letter M should be correctly matched with number 2. In the third pair, the letter D is incorrectly matched with number 2. According to the code table, letter D should be correctly matched with number 4. Since only one of the pairs is correctly matched, the answer to this sample question is B.

23. RSBMRM – 759262
    GDSRVH – 845730
    VDBRTM - 349713

24. TGVSDR – 183247
    SMHRDP – 520647
    TRMHSR - 172057

25. DSPRGM – 456782
    MVDBHT – 234902
    HPMDBT - 062491

26. BVPTRD – 936184
    GDPHMB – 807029
    GMRHMV - 827032

27. MGVRSH – 283750
    TRDMBS – 174295
    SPRMGV - 567283

28. SGBSDM – 489542   28._____
    MGHPTM – 290612
    MPBMHT - 269301

29. TDPBHM – 146902   29._____
    VPBMRS – 369275
    GDMBHM - 842902

30. MVPTBV – 236194   30._____
    PDRTMB – 47128
    BGTMSM - 981232

KEY (CORRECT ANSWERS)

1.	A	11.	B	21.	C
2.	C	12.	C	22.	B
3.	B	13.	D	23.	B
4.	D	14.	D	24.	B
5.	D	15.	D	25.	C
6.	B	16.	C	26.	A
7.	B	17.	D	27.	D
8.	B	18.	A	28.	A
9.	A	19.	B	29.	D
10.	C	20.	A	30.	A

TEST 2

DIRECTIONS: Each question or incomplete statement is followed by several suggested answers or completions. Select the one that BEST answers the question or completes the statement. *PRINT THE LETTER OF THE CORRECT ANSWER IN THE SPACE AT THE RIGHT.*

Questions 1-10.

DIRECTIONS: Questions 1 through 10 each consists of two columns, each containing four lines of names, numbers and/or addresses. For each question, compare the lines in Column I with the lines in Column II to see if they match exactly, and mark your answer A, B, C, or D, according to the following instructions:
- A. all four lines match exactly
- B. only three lines match exactly
- C. only two lines match exactly
- D. only one line matches exactly

<u>COLUMN I</u>　　　　　　　　　　　　　　<u>COLUMN II</u>

1.
   - I. Earl Hodgson
   - II. 1409870
   - III. Shore Ave.
   - IV. Macon Rd.

   - Earl Hodgson
   - 1408970
   - Schore Ave.
   - Macon Rd.

   1.____

2.
   - I. 9671485
   - II. 470 Astor Court
   - III. Halprin, Phillip
   - IV. Frank D. Poliseo

   - 9671485
   - 470 Astor Court
   - Halperin, Phillip
   - Frank D. Poliseo

   2.____

3.
   - I. Tandem Associates
   - II. 144-17 Northern Blvd.
   - III. Alberta Forchi
   - IV. Kings Park, NY 10751

   - Tandom Associates
   - 144-17 Northern Blvd.
   - Albert Forchi
   - Kings Point, NY 10751

   3.____

4.
   - I. Bertha C. McCormack
   - II. Clayton, MO
   - III. 976-4242
   - IV. New City, NY 10951

   - Bertha C. McCormack
   - Clayton, MO
   - 976-4242
   - New City, NY 10951

   4.____

5.
   - I. George C. Morill
   - II. Columbia, SC 29201
   - III. Louis Ingham
   - IV. 3406 Forest Ave.

   - George C. Morrill
   - Columbia, SD 29201
   - Louis Ingham
   - 3406 Forest Ave.

   5.____

6.
   - I. 506 S. Elliott Pl.
   - II. Herbert Hall
   - III. 4712 Rockaway Pkwy
   - IV. 169 E. 7 St.

   - 506 S. Elliott Pl.
   - Hurbert Hall
   - 4712 Rockaway Pkwy
   - 169 E. 7 St.

   6.____

2 (#2)

7.	I.	345 Park Ave.	345 Park Pl.
	II.	Colman Oven Corp.	Coleman Oven Corp.
	III.	Robert Conte	Robert Conti
	IV.	6179846	6179846

7.____

8.	I.	Grigori Schierber	Grigori Schierber
	II.	Des Moines, Iowa	Des Moines, Iowa
	III.	Gouverneur Hospital	Gouverneur Hospital
	IV.	91-35 Cresskill Pl.	91-35 Cresskill Pl.

8.____

9.	I.	Jeffery Janssen	Jeffrey Janssen
	II.	8041071	8041071
	III.	40 Rockefeller Plaza	40 Rockafeller Plaza
	IV.	407 6 St.	406 7 St.

9.____

10.	I.	5971996	5871996
	II.	3113 Knickerbocker Ave.	31123 Knickerbocker Ave.
	III.	8434 Boston Post Rd.	8424 Boston Post Rd.
	IV.	Penn Station	Penn Station

10.____

Questions 11-14.

DIRECTIONS: Questions 11 through 14 are to be answered by looking at the four groups of names and addresses listed below (I, II, III, and IV), and then finding out the number of groups that have their corresponding numbered lies exactly the same.

	GROUP I	GROUP II
Line 1.	Richmond General Hospital	Richman General Hospital
Line 2.	Geriatric Clinic	Geriatric Clinic
Line 3.	3975 Paerdegat St.	3975 Peardegat St.
Line 4.	Loudonville, New York 11538	Londonville, New York 11538

	GROUP III	GROUP IV
Line 1.	Richmond General Hospital	Richmend General Hospital
Line 2.	Geriatric Clinic	Geriatric Clinic
Line 3.	3795 Paerdegat St.	3975 Paerdegat St.
Line 4.	Loudonville, New York 11358	Loudonville, New York 11538

1. In how many groups is line one exactly the same?
   A. Two   B. Three   C. Four   D. None

11.____

12. In how many groups is line two exactly the same?
    A. Two   B. Three   C. Four   D. None

12.____

13. In how many groups is line three exactly the same?
    A. Two   B. Three   C. Four   D. None

13.____

14. In how many groups is line four exactly the same? 14.____
    A. Two   B. Three   C. Four   D. None

Questions 15-18.

DIRECTIONS: Each of Questions 15 through 18 has two lists of names and addresses. Each list contains three sets of names and addresses. Check each of the three sets in the list on the right to see if they are the same as the corresponding set in the list on the left. Mark your answers:
- A. if none of the sets in the right list are the same as those in the left list
- B. if only one of the sets in the right list is the same as those in the left list
- C. if only two of the sets in the right list are the same as those in the left list
- D. if all three sets in the right list are the same as those in the left list

15. Mary T. Berlinger   Mary T. Berlinger   15.____
    2351 Hampton St.   2351 Hampton St.
    Monsey, N.Y. 20117   Monsey, N.Y. 20117

    Eduardo Benes   Eduardo Benes
    483 Kingston Avenue   473 Kingston Avenue
    Central Islip, N.Y. 11734 Central Islip, N.Y. 11734

    Alan Carrington Fuchs   Alan Carrington Fuchs
    17 Gnarled Hollow Road   17 Gnarled Hollow Road
    Los Angeles, CA 91635   Los Angeles, CA 91685

16. David John Jacobson   David John Jacobson   16.____
    178 34 St. Apt. 4C   178 53 St. Apt. 4C
    New York, N.Y. 00927   New York, N.Y. 00927

    Ann-Marie Calonella   Ann-Marie Calonella
    7243 South Ridge Blvd.   7243 South Ridge Blvd.
    Bakersfield, CA 96714   Bakersfield, CA 96714

    Pauline M. Thompson   Pauline M. Thomson
    872 Linden Ave.   872 Linden Ave.
    Houston, Texas 70321   Houston, Texas 70321

17. Chester LeRoy Masterton   Chester LeRoy Masterson   17.____
    152 Lacy Rd.   152 Lacy Rd.
    Kankakee, Ill. 54532   Kankakee, Ill. 54532

    William Maloney   William Maloney
    S. LaCrosse Pla.   S. LaCross Pla.
    Wausau, Wisconsin 52136   Wausau, Wisconsin 52146

    Cynthia V. Barnes   Cynthia V. Barnes
    16 Pines Rd.   16 Pines Rd.
    Greenpoint, Miss. 20376   Greenpoint,, Miss. 20376

4 (#2)

18. Marcel Jean Frontenac   Marcel Jean Frontenac   18.____
     8 Burton On The Water   6 Burton On The Water
     Calender, Me. 01471   Calender, Me. 01471

     J. Scott Marsden   J. Scott Marsden
     174 S. Tipton St.   174 Tipton St.
     Cleveland, Ohio   Cleveland, Ohio

     Lawrence T. Haney   Lawrence T. Haney
     171 McDonough St.   171 McDonough St.
     Decatur, Ga. 31304   Decatur, Ga. 31304

Questions 19-26.

DIRECTIONS: Each of Questions 19 through 26 has two lists of numbers. Each list contains
             three sets of numbers. Check each of the three sets in the list on
             the right to see if they are the same as the corresponding set in the
             list on the left. Mark your answers:
             A. if none of the sets in the right list are the same as those in
                 the left list
             B. if only one of the sets in the right list is the same as those in
                 the left list
             C. if only two of the sets in the right list are the same as those
                 in the left list
             D. if all three sets in the right list are the same as those in the
                 left lists

19. 7354183476   7354983476   19.____
     4474747744   4474747774
     5791430231   57914302311

20. 7143592185   7143892185   20.____
     8344517699   8344518699
     9178531263   9178531263

21. 2572114731   257214731   21.____
     8806835476   8806835476
     8255831246   8255831246

22. 331476853821   331476858621   22.____
     6976658532996   6976655832996
     3766042113715   3766042113745

23. 8806663315   88066633115   23.____
     74477138449   74477138449
     211756663666   211756663666

24. 990006966996   99000696996   24.____
     53022219743   53022219843
     4171171117717   4171171177717

25. 24400222433004   24400222433004   25.____
     5300030055000355 5300030055500355
     20000075532002022 20000075532002022

26. 6111666406600116 61116664066001116   26.____
     7111300117001100733 7111300117001100733
     26666446664476518 26666446664476518

Questions 27-30.

DIRECTIONS: Questions 27 through 30 are to be answered by picking the answer which is in the correct numerical order, from the lowest number to the highest number, in each question.

27. A. 44533, 44518, 44516, 44547   27.____
     B. 44516, 44518, 44533, 44547
     C. 44547, 44533, 44518, 44516
     D. 44518, 44516, 44547, 44533

28. A. 95587, 95593, 95601, 95620   28.____
     B. 95601, 95620, 95587, 95593
     C. 95593, 95587, 95601. 95620
     D. 95620, 95601, 95593, 95587

29. A. 232212, 232208, 232232, 232223   29.____
     B. 232208, 232223, 232212, 232232
     C. 232208, 232212, 232223, 232232
     D. 232223, 232232, 232208, 232208

30. A. 113419, 113521, 113462, 113462   30.____
     B. 113588, 113462, 113521, 113419
     C. 113521, 113588, 113419, 113462
     D. 113419, 113462, 113521, 113588

KEY (CORRECT ANSWERS)

1.	C	11.	A	21.	C
2.	B	12.	C	22.	A
3.	D	13.	A	23.	D
4.	A	14.	A	24.	A
5.	C	15.	C	25.	C
6.	B	16.	B	26.	C
7.	D	17.	B	27.	B
8.	A	18.	B	28.	A
9.	D	19.	B	29.	C
10.	C	20.	B	30.	D

CODING

EXAMINATION SECTION

TEST 1

COMMENTARY

An ingenious question-type called coding, involving elements of alphabetizing, filing, name and number comparison, and evaluative judgment and application, has currently won wide acceptance in testing circles for measuring clerical aptitude and general ability, particularly on the senior (middle) grades (levels).

While the directions for this question-type usually vary in detail, the candidate is generally asked to consider groups of names, codes, and numbers, and, then, according to a given plan, to arrange codes in alphabetic order; to arrange these in numerical sequence; to rearrange columns of names and numbers in correct order; to espy errors in coding; to choose the correct coding arrangement in consonance with the given directions and examples, etc.

This question-type appears to have few parameters in respect to form, substance, or degree of difficulty.

Accordingly, acquaintance with, and practice in the coding question is recommended for the serious candidate.

DIRECTIONS: Column I consists of serial numbers of dollar bills. Column II shows different ways of arranging the corresponding serial numbers.
The serial numbers of dollar bills in Column I begin and end with a capital letter and have an eight-digit number in between. The serial numbers in Column I are to be arranged according to the following rules:
First: In alphabetical order according to the first letter.
Second: When two or more serial numbers have the same first letter, in alphabetical order according to the last letter.
Third: When two or more serial numbers have the same first and last letters, in numerical order, beginning with the lowest number.

The serial numbers in Column I are numbered (1) through (5) in the order in which they are listed. In Column II, the numbers (1) through (5) are arranged in four different ways to show different arrangements of the corresponding serial numbers. Choose the answer in Column II in which the serial numbers are arranged according to the above rules.

Column I

1. E75044127B
2. B96399104A
3. B93939086A
4. B47064465H

Column II

A. 4, 1, 3, 2, 5
B. 4, 1, 2, 3, 5
C. 4, 3, 2, 5, 1
D. 3, 2, 5, 4, 1

In the simple question, the four serial numbers starting with B should be put before the serial number starting with E. The serial numbers starting with B and ending with A should be put before the serial number starting with B and ending with H. The three serial numbers starting with B and ending with A should be listed in numerical order, beginning with the lowest number. The correct way to arrange the serial numbers, therefore, is:

    3. B93939086A
    2. B96399104A
    5. B99040922A
    4. B47064465H
    1. E75044127B

Since the order of arrangement is 3, 2, 5, 4, 1, the answer to the sample question is D.

	Column I	Column II	
1.	1. D89143888P 2. D98143838B 3. D89113883B 4. D89148338P 5. D89148388B	A. 3, 5, 2, 1, 4 B. 3, 1, 4, 5, 2 C. 4, 2, 3, 1, 5 D. 4, 1, 3, 5, 2	1.____
2.	1. W62455590E 2. W62455090F 3. W62405099E 4. V62455097F 5. V62405979E	A. 2, 4, 3, 1, 5 B. 3, 1, 5, 2, 4 C. 5, 3, 1, 4, 2 D. 5, 4, 3, 1, 2	2.____
3.	1. N74663826M 2. M74633286M 3. N76633228N 4. M76483686N 5. M74636688M	A. 2, 4, 5, 3, 1 B. 2, 5, 4, 1, 3 C. 1, 2, 5, 3, 4 D. 2, 5, 1, 4, 3	3.____
4.	1. P97560324B 2. R97663024B 3. P97503024E 4. R97563240E 5. P97652304B	A. 1, 5, 2, 3, 4 B. 3, 1, 4, 5, 2 C. 1, 5, 3, 2, 4 D. 1, 5, 2, 3, 4	4.____
5.	1. H92411165G 2. A92141465G 3. H92141165C 4. H92444165C 5. A92411465G	A. 2, 5, 3, 4, 1 B. 3, 4, 2, 5, 1 C. 3, 2, 1, 5, 4 D. 3, 1, 2, 5, 4	5.____
6.	1. X90637799S 2. N90037696S 3. Y90677369B 4. X09677693B 5. M09673699S	A. 4, 3, 5, 2, 1 B. 5, 4, 2, 1, 3 C. 5, 2, 4, 1, 3 D. 5, 2, 3, 4, 1	6.____

	Column I	Column II	
7.	1. K78425174L 2. K78452714C 3. K78547214N 4. K78442774C 5. K78547724M	A. 4, 2, 1, 3, 5 B. 2, 3, 5, 4, 1 C. 1, 4, 2, 3, 5 D. 4, 2, 1, 5, 3	7.____
8.	1. P18736652U 2. P18766352V 3. T17686532U 4. T17865523U 5. P18675332V	A. 1, 3, 4, 5, 2 B. 1, 5, 2, 3, 4 C. 3, 4, 5, 1, 2 D. 5, 2, 1, 3, 4	8.____
9.	1. L51138101K 2. S51138001R 3. S51188222K 4. S51183110R 5. L51188100R	A. 1, 5, 3, 2, 4 B. 1, 3, 5, 2, 4 C. 1, 5, 1, 4, 3 D. 2, 5, 1, 4, 3	9.____
10.	1. J28475336 2. T28775363D 3. J27843566P 4. T27834563P 5. J2843553D	A. 5, 1, 2, 3, 4 B. 4, 3, 5, 1, 2 C. 1, 5, 2, 4, 3 D. 5, 1, 3, 2, 4	10.____
11.	1. S55126179E 2. R51336177Q 3. P55126177R 4. S55126178R 5. R55126180P	A. 1, 5, 2, 3, 4 B. 3, 4, 1, 5, 2 C. 3, 5, 2, 1, 4 D. 4, 3, 1, 5, 2	11.____
12.	1. T64217813Q 2. I64217817O 3. T64217818O 4. I64217811Q 5. T64217816Q	A. 4, 1, 3, 2, 4 B. 2, 4, 3, 1, 5 C. 4, 1, 5, 2, 3 D. 2, 3, 4, 1, 5	12.____
13.	1. B33886897B 2. B38386882B 3. D33389862B 4. D33336887D 5. B38888697D	A. 5, 1, 3, 4, 2 B. 1, 2, 5, 3, 4 C. 1, 2, 5, 4, 3 D. 2, 1, 4, 5, 3	13.____
14.	1. E11664554M 2. F11164544M 3. F11614455N 4. E11665454M 5. F16161545N	A. 4, 1, 2, 5, 3 B. 2, 4, 1, 5, 3 C. 4, 2, 1, 3, 5 D. 1, 4, 2, 3, 5	14.____

4 (#1)

	Column I	Column II	
15.	1. C86611355W 2. C68631533V 3. G88631533V 4. C68833515V 5. G68833511W	A. 2, 4, 1, 5, 3 B. 1, 2, 4, 3, 5 C. 1, 2, 5, 4, 3 D. 1, 2, 4, 3, 5	15.____
16.	1. R73665312J 2. P73685512J 3. P73968511J 4. R73665321K 5. R63985211K	A. 3, 2, 1, 4, 5 B. 2, 3, 5, 1, 4 C. 2, 3, 1, 5, 4 D. 3, 1, 5, 2, 4	16.____
17.	1. X33661222U 2. Y83961323V 3. Y88991123V 4. X33691233U 5. X38691333U	A. 1, 4, 5, 2, 3 B. 4, 5, 1, 3, 2 C. 4, 5, 1, 2, 3 D. 4, 1, 5, 2, 3	17..____
18.	1. B22838847W 2. B28833874V 3. B22288344X 4. B28238374V 5. B28883347V	A. 4, 5, 2, 3, 1 B. 4, 2, 5, 1, 3 C. 4, 5, 2, 1, 3 D. 4, 1, 5, 2, 3	18.____
19.	1. H44477447G 2. H47444777G 3. H74777477C 4. H44747447G 5. H77747447C	A. 1, 3, 5, 4, 2 B. 3, 1, 5, 2, 4 C. 1, 4, 2, 3, 5 D. 3, 5, 1, 4, 2	19.____
20.	1. G11143447G 2. G15133388C 3. C15134378G 4. G11534477C 5. C15533337C	A. 3, 5, 1, 4, 2 B. 1, 4, 3, 2, 5 C. 5, 3, 4, 2, 1 D. 4, 3, 1, 2, 5	20.____
21.	1. J96693369F 2. J66939339F 3. J96693693E 4. J966T3933E 5. J69639363F	A. 4, 3, 2, 5, 1 B. 2, 5, 4, 1, 3 C. 2, 5, 4, 3, 1 D. 3, 4, 5, 2, 1	21.____
22.	1. L15567834Z 2. P11587638Z 3. M51567688Z 4. O55578784Z 5. N53588783Z	A. 3, 1, 5, 2, 4 B. 1, 3, 5, 4, 2 C. 1, 3, 5, 2, 4 D. 3, 1, 4, 4, 2	22.____

5 (#1)

	Column I	Column II	

23.
1. C83261824G
2. C78361822C
3. G83261732G
4. C88261823C
5. G83261743C

A. 2, 4, 1, 5, 3
B. 4, 2, 1, 3, 5
C. 3, 1, 5, 2, 4
D. , 3, 5, 1, 4

23.____

24.
1. A11710107H
2. H17110017A
3. A11170707A
4. H17170171H
5. A11710177A

A. 2, 1, 4, 3, 5
B. 3, 1, 5, 2, 4
C. 3, 4, 1, 5, 2
D. 3, 5, 1, 2, 4

24.____

25.
1. R26794821S
2. O26794821T
3. M26794821Z
4. Q26794821R
5. S26794821P

A. 3, 2, 4, 1, 5
B. 3, 4, 2, 1, 5
C. 4, 2, 1, 3, 5
D. 5, 4, 1, 2, 3

25.____

KEY (CORRECT ANSWERS)

1. A
2. D
3. B
4. C
5. A

6. C
7. D
8. B
9. A
10. D

11. C
12. B
13. B
14. D
15. A

16. C
17. A
18. B
19. D
20. C

21. A
22. B
23. A
24. D
25. A

TEST 2

Questions 1-5.

DIRECTIONS: Questions 1 through 5 consist of a set of letters and numbers located under Column I. For each question, pick the answer (A, B, C, or D) located under Column II which contains ONLY letters and numbers that appear in the question in Column II. *PRINT THE LETTER OF THE CORRECT ANSWER IN THE SPACE AT THE RIGHT.*

SAMPLE QUESTION

Column I

B-9-P-H-2-Z-N-8-4-M

Column II

A. B-4-C-3-R-9
B. 4-H-P-8-6-N
C. P-2-Z-8-M-9
D. 4-B-N-5-E-Z

Choice C is the correct answer because P,2,Z,8,M and 9 all appear in the sample question. All the other choices have at least one letter or number that is not in the question.

Column I

1. 1-7-6-J-L-T-3-S-A-2

2. C-0-Q-5-3-9-H-L-2-7

3. P-3-B-C-5-6-0-E-1-T

4. U-T-Z-2-4-S-8-6-B-3

5. 4-D-F-G-C-6-8-3-J-L

Column II

1.
A. J-3-S-A-7-L
B. T-S-A-2-6-5
C. 3-7-J-L-S-Z
D. A-7-4-J-L-1

2.
A. F-9-T-2-7-Q
B. 3-0-6-9-L-C
C. 9-L-7-Q-C-3
D. H-Q-4-5-9-7

3.
A. B-4-6-1-3-T
B. T-B-P-3-E-0
C. 5-3-0-E-B-G
D. 0-6-P-T-9-B

4.
A. 2-4-S-V-Z-3
B. B-Z-S-8-3-6
C. 4-T-U-8-L-B
D. 9-3-T-Z-1-2

5.
A. T-D-6-8-4-J
B. C-4-3-2-J-F
C. 8-3-C-5-G-6
D. C-8-6-J-G-L

1.____

2.____

3.____

4.____

5.____

Questions 6-12.

DIRECTIONS: Each of the questions numbered 6 through 12 consist of a long series of letters and numbers under Column I and four short series of letters and numbers under Column II. For each question, choose the short series of letters and numbers which is entirely and exactly the same as some part of the long series.

	Column I		Column II	
6.	IE227FE383L4700	A. B. C. D.	E27FE3 EF838L EL4700 83LE70	6.____
7.	77J646G54NPB318	A. B. C. D.	NPB318 J646J5 4G54NP C54NPB	7.____
8.	85887T358W24A93	A. B. C. D.	858887 W24A93 858W24 87T353	8.____
9.	E104RY796B33H14	A. B. C. D.	04RY79 E14RYR 96B3H1 RY7996	9.____
10.	W58NP12141DE07M	A. B. C. D.	8MP121 W58NP1 14DEO7 12141D	10.____
11.	P473R365M442V5W	A. B. C. D.	P47365 73P365 365M44 5X42V5	11.____
12.	865CG441V21SS59	A. B. C. D.	1V12SS V21SS5 5GC441 894CG4	12.____

KEY (CORRECT ANSWERS)

1.	A	7.	A
2.	C	8.	B
3.	B	9.	A
4.	B	10.	D
5.	D	11.	C
6	D	12.	B

TEST 3

DIRECTIONS: Each question from 1 through 8 consists of a set of letters and numbers. For each question, pick as your answer from the column to the right the choice has ONLY numbers and letters that are in the question you are answering.

To help you understand what to do, the following sample question is given:

SAMPLE: B-9-P-H-2-Z-N-8-4-M
    A. B-4-C-3-E-9
    B. 4-H-P-8-6-N
    C. P-2-Z-8-M-9
    D. 4-B-N-R-E-A

Choice C is the correct answer because P, 2, Z, 8, M-9 are in the sample question. All the other choices have at least one letter or number that is not in the question.

Questions 1 through 4 are based on Column I.

Column I

1. X-8-3-I-H-9-4-G-P-U   A. I-G-W-8-2-1   1.____

2. 4-1-2-X-U-B-9-H-7-3   B. U-3-G-9-P-8   2.____

3. U-I-G-2-5-4-W-P-3-B   C. 3-G-I-4-S-U   3.____

4. 3-H-7-G-4-5-1-U-B   D. 9-X-4-7-2-H   4.____

Questions 5 through 8 are based on Column II.

Column II

5. L-2-9-Z-R-8-Q-Y-5-7   A. 8-R-N-3-T-Z   5.____

6. J-L-9-N-Y-8-5-Q-Z-2   B. 2-L-R-5-7-Q   6.____

7. T-Y-3-3-J-Q-2-N-R-Z   C. J-2-8-Z-T-5   7.____

8. 8-Z-7-T-N-L-1-E-R-3   D. Z-8-9-3-L-5   8.____

KEY (CORRECT ANSWERS)

1. B 5. B
2. D 6. C
3. C 7. A
4. C 8. A

TEST 4

DIRECTIONS: Questions 1 through 5 have lines of letters and numbers. Each letter should be matched with its number in accordance with the following table.

Letter:	F	R	C	A	W	L	E	N	B	T
Matching Number:	0	1	2	3	4	5	6	7	8	9

From the table you can determine that the letter F has the matching number 0 below it, the letter R has the matching number 1 below it, etc.

For each question, compare each line of letters and numbers carefully to see if each letter has its correct matching number. If all the letters and numbers are matched correctly in none of the line of the question, mark your answer A; only one of the lines in the question, mark your answer B; only two of the lines of the question, mark your answer C; all three lines of the question, mark your answer D.

```
WBCR    4826
TLBF    9580
ATNE    3986
```

There is a mistake in the first line because the letter R should have its matching number 1 instead of the number 6. The second line is correct because each letter shown has the correct matching number.

There is a mistake in the third line because the letter N should have the matching number 7 instead of the number 8. Since all the letters and numbers are matched correctly in only one of the lines in the sample, the correct answer is B.

1. EBCT   6829   1._____
    ATWR   3962
    NLBW   7584

2. RNCT   1729   2._____
    LNCR   5728
    WAEB   5368

3. STWB   7948   3._____
    RABL   1385
    TAEF   9360

4. LWRB   5417   4._____
    RLWN   1647
    CBWA   2843

5. ABTC   3792   5._____
    WCER   5261
    AWCN   3417

KEY (CORRECT ANSWERS)

1. C
2. B
3. D
4. B
5. A

TEST 5

DIRECTIONS: Assume that each of the capital letters in the table below represents the name of an employee enrolled in the city employees' retirement system. The number directly beneath the letter represents the agency for which the employee works, and the small letter directly beneath represents the code for the employee's account.

Name of Employee:	L	O	T	Q	A	M	R	N	C
Agency:	3	4	5	9	8	7	52	1	6
Account Code:	r	f	b	i	d	t	g	e	n

In each of the following Questions 1 through 10, the agency code numbers and the account code letters in Columns 2 and 3 should correspond to the capital letters in Column 1 and should be in the same consecutive order. For each question, look at each column carefully and mark your answer as follows:
    if there are one or more errors in Column 2 only, mark your answer A;
    if there are one or more errors in Column 3 only, mark your answer B;
    if there are one or more error in Column 2 and one or more errors in Column 3, mark your answer C;
    if there are NO errors in either column, mark your answer D.

The following sample question is given to help you understand the procedure.

Column 1	Column 2	Column 3
TQLMOC	583746	birtfn

In Column 2, the second agency code number (corresponding to letter Q) should be "9," not "8." Column 3 is coded correctly to Column 1. Since there is an error only in Column 2, the correct answer is A.

	Column 1	Column 2	Column 3	
1.	QLNRCA	931268	ifegnd	1.____
2.	NRMOTC	127546	egftbn	2.____
3.	RCTALM	265837	gndbrt	3.____
4.	TAMLON	578341	bdtrfe	4.____
5.	ANTROM	815427	debigt	5.____
6.	MRALON	728341	tgdrfe	6.____
7.	CTNQRO	657924	ndeigf	7.____
8.	QMROTA	972458	itgfbd	8.____

99

2 (#5)

	Column 1	Column 2	Column 3	
9.	RQMCOL	297463	gitnfr	9._____
10.	NOMRTQ	147259	eftgbi	10._____

KEY (CORRECT ANSWERS)

1. D
2. C
3. B
4. A
5. B
6. D
7. C
8. D
9. A
10. D

TEST 6

DIRECTIONS: Each of Questions 1 through 6 consist of three lines of code letters and numbers. The numbers on each line should correspond to the code letter on the same line in accordance with the table below.

Code Letter:	D	Y	K	L	P	U	S	R	A	E
Corresponding Number:	0	1	2	3	4	5	6	7	8	9

On some of the lines an error exists in the coding. Prepare the letters and numbers in each question carefully. If you find an error or errors on
   only one of the lines in the question, mark your answer A;
   any two lines in the question, mark your answer B;
   all three lines in the question, mark your answer C;
   none of the lines in the question, mark your answer D.

SAMPLE QUESTION
   KSRYELD   2671930
   SAPUEKL   6845913
   RYKADLP   5128034

In the above sample, the first line is correct since each code letter listed has the correct corresponding number. On the second line, an error exists because code letter R should have the number 2 instead of number 1. On the third line, an error exists because the code letter R should have the number 7 instead of the number 5. Since there are errors on two of the three lines, the correct answer is B.

Now answer the following questions using the same procedure.

1. YPUSRLD   1456730
    UPSAEDY   5648901
    PREYDKS   4791026

2. AERLPUS   8973456
    DKLYDPA   0231048
    UKLDREP   5230794

3. DAPUSLA   0845683
    YKLDLPS   1230356
    PUSKYDE   4562101

4. LRPUPDL   3745403
    SUPLEDR   6543907
    PKEYDLU   4291025

5. KEYDESR   2910967
    PRSALEY   4678391
    LRAYSK   3687162

2 (#6)

6. YESREYL   1967913   6._____
   PLPRAKY   4346821
   YLPSRDU   1346705

KEY (CORRECT ANSWERS)

1. A   4. A
2. D   5. B
3. C   6. A

NAME AND NUMBER CHECKING
EXAMINATION SECTION
TEST 1

DIRECTIONS: Questions 1 through 17 consist of sets of names and addresses. In each question, the name and address in Column II should be an exact copy of the name and address in Column I.
If there is:
a mistake only in the name, mark your answer A;
a mistake only in the address, mark your answer B;
a mistake in both name and address, mark your answer C;
No mistake in either name or address, mark your answer D.

Sample Question

Column I
Christina Magnusson
288 Greene Street
New York, N.Y. 10003

Column II
Christina Magnusson
288 Greene Street
New York, N.Y. 10013

Since there is a mistake only in the address (the zip code should be 10003 instead of 10013), the answer to the sample question is B.

COLUMN I

1. Ms. Joan Kelly
313 Franklin Avenue
Brooklyn, N.Y. 11202

2. Mrs. Eileen Engel
47-24 86 Road
Queens, N.Y. 11122

3. Marcia Michaels
213 E. 81 St.
New York, N.Y. 10012

4. Rev. Edward J. Smyth
1401 Brandeis Street
San Francisco, Calif. 96201

5. Alicia Rodriguez
24-68 82 St.
Elmhurst, N.Y. 11122

COLUMN II

1. Ms. Joan Kielly
318 Franklin Ave.
Brooklyn, N.Y. 11202

2. Mrs. Ellen Engel
47-24 86 Road
Queens, New York 11122

3. Marcia Michaels
213 E. 81 St.
New York, N.Y. 10012

4. Rev. Edward J. Smyth
1401 Brandies Street
San Francisco, Calif. 96201

5. Alicia Rodriguez
2468 81 St.
Elmhurst, N.Y. 11122

1.____
2.____
3.____
4.____
5.____

COLUMN I	COLUMN II	
6. Ernest Eisemann 21 Columbia St. New York, N.Y. 10007	Ernest Eisermann 21 Columbia St. New York, N.Y. 10007	6.____
7. Mr. & Mrs. George Petersson 87-11 91st Avenue Woodhaven, N.Y. 11421	Mr. & Mrs. George Peterson 87-11 91st Avenue Woodhaven, N.Y. 11421	7.____
8. Mr. Ivan Klebnikov 1848 Newkirk Avenue Brooklyn, N.Y. 11226	Mr. Ivan Klebikov 1848 Newkirk Avenue Brooklyn, N.Y. 11622	8.____
9. Mr. Samuel Rothfleisch 71 Pine Street New York, N.Y. 10005	Samuel Rothfleisch 71 Pine Street New York, N.Y. 100005	9.____
10. Mrs. Isabel Tonnessen 198 East 185th Street Bronx, N.Y. 10458	Mrs. Isabel Tonnessen 189 East 185th Street Bronx, N.Y. 10348	10.____
11. Esteban Perez 173 Eighth Street Staten Island, N.Y. 10306	Estaban Perez 173 Eighth Street Staten Island, N.Y. 10306	11.____
12. Esta Wong 141 West 68 St. New York, N.Y. 10023	Esta Wang 141 West 68 St. New York, N.Y. 10023	12.____
13. Dr. Alberto Grosso 3475 12th Avenue Brooklyn, N.Y. 11218	Dr. Alberto Grosso 3475 12th Avenue Brooklyn, N.Y. 11218	13.____
14. Mrs. Ruth Bortias 482 Theresa Ct. Far Rockaway, N.Y. 11691	Ms. Ruth Bortlas 482 Theresa Ct. Far Rockaway, N.Y. 11169	14.____
15. Mr. & Mrs. Howard Fox 2301 Sedgwick Ave. Bronx, N.Y. 10468	Mr. & Mrs. Howard Fox 231 Sedgwick Ave. Bronx, N.Y. 10468	15.____
16. Miss Marjorie Black 223 East 23 Street New York, N.Y. 10010	Miss Margorie Black 223 East 23 Street New York, N.Y. 10010	16.____

3 (#1)

COLUMN I	COLUMN II	
17. Michelle Herman 806 Valley Rd. Old Tappan, N.J. 07675	Michelle Hermann 806 Valley Dr. Old Tappan, N.J. 07675	17.____

KEY (CORRECT ANSWERS)

1.	C	7.	A	13.	D
2.	A	8.	C	14.	C
3.	D	9.	D	15.	B
4.	B	10.	B	16.	A
5.	B	11.	A	17.	C
6.	A	12.	D		

TEST 2

DIRECTIONS: Questions 1 through 15 are to be answered SOLELY on the instructions given below. *PRINT THE LETTER OF THE CORRECT ANSWER IN THE SPACE AT THE RIGHT.*

INSTRUCTIONS

In each of the following questions, the 3-line name and address in Column I is the masterlist entry, and the 3-line entry in Column II is the information to be checked against the master list. If there is one line that does not match, mark your answer A; if there are two lines that do not match, mark your answer B; if all three lines do not match, mark your answer C; if the lines all match exactly, mark your answer D.

Sample Question

Column I
Mark L. Field
11-09 Price Park Blvd.
Bronx, N.Y. 11402

Column II
Mark L. Field
11-99 Prince Park Way
Bronx, N.Y. 11401

The first lines in each column match exactly. The second lines do not match since 11-09 does not match 11-<u>99</u>; and Blvd. does not match <u>Way</u>. The third lines do not match either since 1140<u>2</u> does not match 1140<u>1</u>. Therefore, there are two lines that do not match, and the CORRECT answer is B.

COLUMN I	COLUMN II	
1. Jerome A. Jackson 1243 14th Avenue New York, N.Y. 10023	Jerome A. Johnson 1234 14th Avenue New York, N.Y. 10023	1.____
2. Sophie Strachtheim 33-28 Connecticut Ave. Far Rockaway, N.Y. 11697	Sophie Strachtheim 33-28 Connecticut Ave. Far Rockaway, N.Y. 11697	2.____
3. Elisabeth N.T. Gorrell 256 Exchange St. New York, N.Y. 10013	Elizabeth N.T. Gorrell 256 Exchange St. New York, N.Y. 10013	3.____
4. Maria J. Gonzalez 7516 E. Sheepshead Rd. Brooklyn, N.Y. 11240	Maria J. Gonzalez 7516 N. Shepshead Rd. Brooklyn, N.Y. 11240	4.____
5. Leslie B. Brautenweiler 21 57A Seiler Terr. Flushing, N.Y. 11367	Leslie B. Brautenwieler 21-75A Seiler Terr. Flushing, N.J. 11367	5.____

2 (#2)

COLUMN I	COLUMN II	
6. Rigoberto J. Peredes 157 Twin Towers, #18F Tottenville, S. I., N.Y,	Rigoberto J. Peredes 157 Twin Towers, #18F Tottenville, S.I., N.Y.	6.____
7. Pietro F. Albino P.O. Box 7548 Floral Park, N.Y. 11005	Pietro F. Albina P.O. Box 7458 Floral Park, N.Y. 11005	7.____
8. Joanne Zimmerman Bldg. SW, Room 314 532-4601	Joanne Zimmermann Bldg. SW, Room 314 532-4601	8.____
9. Carlyle Whetstone Payroll Div. –A, Room 212A 262-5000, ext. 471	Carlyle Whetstone Payroll Div. –A, Room 212A 262-5000, ext. 417	9.____
10. Kenneth Chiang Legal Council, Room 9745 (201) 416-9100, ext. 17	Kenneth Chiang Legal Counsel, Room 9745 (201) 416-9100, Ext. 17	10.____
11. Ethel Koenig Personnel Services Division, Room 433; 635-7572	Ethel Hoenig Personal Services Division, Room 433; 635-7527	11.____
12. Joyce Ehrhardt Office of the Administrator, Room W56; 387-8706	Joyce Ehrhart Office of the Administrator, Room W56; 387-7806	12.____
13. Ruth Lang EAM Bldg., Room C101 625-2000, ext. 765	Ruth Lang EAM Bldg., Room C110 625-2000, ext. 765	13.____
14. Anne Marie Ionozzi Investigations, Room 827 576-4000, ext. 832	Anna Marie Ionozzi Investigation, Room 827 566-4000, ext. 832	14.____
15. Willard Jameson Fm C Bldg., Room 687 454-3010	Willard Jamieson Fm C Bldg., Room 687 454-3010	15.____

KEY (CORRECT ANSWERS)

1.	B	6.	D	11.	C
2.	D	7.	B	12.	B
3.	A	8.	D	13.	A
4.	A	9.	B	14.	C
5.	C	10.	A	15.	A

TEST 3

DIRECTIONS: Questions 1 through 10 are to be answered on the basis of the following instructions. *PRINT THE LETTER OF THE CORRECT ANSWER IN THE SPACE AT THE RIGHT.*

<u>INSTRUCTIONS</u>

For each such set of names, addresses, and numbers listed in Columns I and II, select your answer from the following options:
- The names in Columns I and II are different,
- The addresses in Columns I and II are different,
- The numbers in Columns I and II are different,
- The names, addresses, and numbers in Columns I and II are identical.

<u>COLUMN I</u>   <u>COLUMN II</u>

1. Francis Jones   Francis Jones   1.____
   62 Stately Avenue   62 Stately Avenue
   96-12446   96-21446

2. Julio Montez   Julio Montez   2.____
   19 Ponderosa Road   19 Ponderosa Road
   56-73161   56-71361

3. Mary Mitchell   Mary Mitchell   3.____
   2314 Melbourne Drive   2314 Melbourne Drive
   68-92172   68-92172

4. Harry Patterson   Harry Patterson   4.____
   25 Dunne Street   25 Dunne Street
   14-33430   14-34330

5. Patrick Murphy   Patrick Murphy   5.____
   171 West Hosmer Street   171 West Hosmer Street
   93-81214   93-18214

6. August Schultz   August Schultz   6.____
   816 St. Clair Avenue   816 St. Claire Avenue
   53-40149   53-40149

7. George Taft   George Taft   7.____
   72 Runnymede Street   72 Runnymede Street
   47-04033   47-04023

8. Angus Henderson   Angus Henderson   8.____
   1418 Madison Street   1318 Madison Street
   81-76375   81-76375

COLUMN I	COLUMN II	
9. Carolyn Mazur 12 Riverview Road 38-99615	Carolyn Mazur 12 Rivervane Road 38-99615	9.____
10. Adele Russell 1725 Lansing Lane 72-91962	Adela Russell 1725 Lansing Lane 72-91962	10.____

KEY (CORRECT ANSWERS)

1.	C	6.	B
2.	C	7.	C
3.	D	8.	D
4.	C	9.	B
5.	C	10.	A

TEST 4

DIRECTIONS: Questions 1 through 20 test how good you are at catching mistakes in typing or printing. In each question, the name and address in Column II should be an exact copy of the name and address in Column I. Mark your answer
- A. If there is no mistake in either name or address;
- B. If there is a mistake in both name and address;
- C. If there is a mistake only in the name;
- D. If there is a mistake only in the address.

PRINT THE LETTER OF THE CORRECT ANSWER IN THE SPACE AT THE RIGHT.

COLUMN I	COLUMN II	
1. Milos Yanocek 33-60 14 Street Long Island City, N.Y. 11011	Milos Yanocek 33-60 14 Street Long Island City, N.Y. 11001	1.____
2. Alphonse Sabattelo 24 Minnetta Lane New York, N.Y. 10006	Alphonse Sabbattelo 24 Minetta Lane New York, N.Y. 10006	2.____
3. Helen Steam 5 Metropolitan Oval Bronx, N.Y. 10462	Helene Stearn 5 Metropolitan Oval Bronx, N.Y. 10462	3.____
4. Jacob Weisman 231 Francis Lewis Boulevard Forest Hills, N.Y. 11325	Jacob Weisman 231 Francis Lewis Boulevard Forest Hills, N.Y. 11325	4.____
5. Riccardo Fuente 134 West 83 Street New York, N.Y. 10024	Riccardo Fuentes 134 West 88 Street New York, N.Y. 10024	5.____
6. Dennis Lauber 52 Avenue D Brooklyn, N.Y. 11216	Dennis Lauder 52 Avenue D Brooklyn, N.Y. 11216	6.____
7. Paul Cutter 195 Galloway Avenue Staten Island, N.Y. 10356	Paul Cutter 175 Galloway Avenue Staten Island, N.Y. 10365	7.____
8. Sean Donnelly 45-58 41 Avenue Woodside, N.Y. 11168	Sean Donnelly 45-58 41 Avenue Woodside, N.Y. 11168	8.____
9. Clyde Willot 1483 Rockaway Avenue Brooklyn, N.Y. 11238	Clyde Willat 1483 Rockaway Avenue Brooklyn, N.Y. 11238	9.____

2 (#4)

COLUMN I	COLUMN II	
10. Michael Stanakis 419 Sheriden Avenue Staten Island, N.Y. 10363	Michael Stanakis 419 Sheraden Avenue Staten Island, N.Y. 10363	10.____
11. Joseph DiSilva 63-84 Saunders Road Rego Park, N.Y. 11431	Joseph Disilva 64-83 Saunders Road Rego Park, N.Y. 11431	11.____
12. Linda Polansky 2224 Fendon Avenue Bronx, N.Y. 20464	Linda Polansky 2255 Fenton Avenue Bronx, N.Y. 10464	12.____
13. Alfred Klein 260 Hillside Terrace Staten Island, N.Y. 15545	Alfred Klein 260 Hillside Terrace Staten Island, N.Y. 15545	13.____
14. William McDonnell 504 E. 55 Street New York, N.Y. 10103	William McConnell 504 E. 55 Street New York, N.Y. 10108	14.____
15. Angela Cipolla 41-11 Parson Avenue Flushing, N.Y. 11446	Angela Cipola 41-11 Parsons Avenue Flushing, N.Y. 11446	15.____
16. Julie Sheridan 1212 Ocean Avenue Brooklyn, N.Y. 11237	Julia Sheridan 1212 Ocean Avenue Brooklyn, N.Y. 11237	16.____
17. Arturo Rodriguez 2156 Cruger Avenue Bronx, N.Y. 10446	Arturo Rodrigues 2156 Cruger Avenue Bronx, N.Y. 10446	17.____
18. Helen McCabe 2044 East 19 Street Brooklyn, N.Y. 11204	Helen McCabe 2040 East 19 Street Brooklyn, N.Y. 11204	18.____
19. Charles Martin 526 West 160 Street New York, N.Y. 10022	Charles Martin 526 West 160 Street New York, N.Y. 10022	19.____
20. Morris Rabinowitz 31 Avenue M Brooklyn, N.Y. 11216	Morris Rabinowitz 31 Avenue N Brooklyn, N.Y. 11216	20.____

KEY (CORRECT ANSWERS)

1.	D	11.	B
2.	B	12.	D
3.	C	13.	A
4.	A	14.	B
5.	B	15.	B
6.	C	16.	C
7.	D	17.	C
8.	A	18.	D
9.	B	19.	A
10.	D	20.	D

TEST 5

DIRECTIONS: In copying the addresses below from Column A to the same line in Column B, an Agent-in-Training made some errors. For Questions 1 through 5, if you find that the agent made an error in
only one line, mark your answer A;
only two lines, mark your answer B;
only three lines, mark your answer C;
all four lines, mark your answer D.

EXAMPLE

COLUMN A	COLUMN B
24 Third Avenue	24 Third Avenue
5 Lincoln Road	5 Lincoln Street
50 Central Park West	6 Central Park West
37-21 Queens Boulevard	21-37 Queens Boulevard

Since errors were made on only three lines, namely the second, third, and fourth, the CORRECT answer is C.
PRINT THE LETTER OF THE CORRECT ANSWER IN THE SPACE AT THE RIGHT.

	COLUMN A	COLUMN B	
1.	57-22 Springfield Boulevard 94 Gun Hill Road 8 New Dorp Lane 36 Bedford Avenue	75-22 Springfield Boulevard 94 Gun Hill Avenue 8 New Drop Lane 36 Bedford Avenue	1.____
2.	538 Castle Hill Avenue 54-15 Beach Channel Drive 21 Ralph Avenue 162 Madison Avenue	538 Castle Hill Avenue 54-15 Beach Channel Drive 21 Ralph Avenue 162 Morrison Avenue	2.____
3.	49 Thomas Street 27-21 Northern Blvd. 86 125th Street 872 Atlantic Ave.	49 Thomas Street 21-27 Northern Blvd. 86 125th Street 872 Baltic Ave,	3.____
4.	261-17 Horace Harding Expwy. 191 Fordham Road 6 Victory Blvd. 552 Oceanic Ave.	261-17 Horace Harding Pkwy. 191 Fordham Road 6 Victoria Blvd. 552 Ocean Ave.	4.____
5.	90-05 38th Avenue 19 Central Park West 9281 Avenue X 22 West Farms Square	90-05 36th Avenue 19 Central Park East 9281 Avenue X 22 West Farms Square	5.____

KEY (CORRECT ANSWERS)

1. C
2. A
3. B
4. C
5. B

TEST 6

DIRECTIONS: For Questions 1 through 10, choose the letter in Column II next to the number which EXACTLY matches the number in Column I. *PRINT THE LETTER OF THE CORRECT ANSWER IN THE SPACE AT THE RIGHT.*

COLUMN I COLUMN II

1. 14235
   - A. 13254
   - B. 12435
   - C. 13245
   - D. 14235

   1.____

2. 70698
   - A. 90768
   - B. 60978
   - C. 70698]
   - D. 70968

   2.____

3. 11698
   - A. 11689
   - B. 11986
   - C. 11968
   - D. 11698

   3.____

4. 50497
   - A. 50947
   - B. 50497
   - C. 50749
   - D. 54097

   4.____

5. 69635
   - A. 60653
   - B. 69630
   - C. 69365
   - D. 69635

   5.____

6. 1201022011
   - A. 1201022011
   - B. 1201020211
   - C. 1202012011
   - D. 1021202011

   6.____

7. 3893981389
   - A. 3893891389
   - B. 3983981389
   - C. 3983891389
   - D. 3893981389

   7.____

8. 4765476589
   - A. 4765476598
   - B. 4765476588
   - C. 4765476589
   - D. 4765746589

   8.____

9. 8679678938
    A. 8679687938
    B. 8679678938
    C. 8697678938
    D. 8678678938

    9.____

10. 6834836932
    A. 6834386932
    B. 6834836923
    C. 6843836932
    D. 6834836932

    10.____

Questions 11-15.

DIRECTIONS: For Questions 11 through 15, determine how many of the symbols in Column Z are exactly the same as the symbol in Column Y.
If none is exactly the same, answer A;
If only one symbol is exactly the same, answer B;
If two symbols are exactly the same, answer C;
If three symbols are exactly the same, answer D.

COLUMN Y	COLUMN Z	
11. A123B1266	A123B1366 A123B1266 A133B1366 A123B1266	11.____
12. CC28D3377	CD22D3377 CC38D3377 CC28C3377 CC28D2277	12.____
13. M21AB201X	M12AB201X M21AB201X M21AB201Y M21BA201X	13.____
14. PA383Y744	AP383Y744 PA338Y744 PA388Y744 PA383Y774	14.____
15. PB2Y8893	PB2Y8893 PB2Y8893 PB3Y8898 PB2Y8893	15.____

KEY (CORRECT ANSWERS)

1.	D	6.	A	11.	C
2.	C	7.	D	12.	A
3.	D	8.	C	13.	B
4.	B	9.	B	14.	A
5.	D	10.	D	15.	D

VEHICLE AND TRAFFIC LAW (V&T)

TABLE OF CONTENTS

	Page
I. PROVISIONS	1
A. Traffic Infractions	1
B. Abandoned Vehicles	1
C. Arrests and Traffic Tickets	1
D. Traffic Information or Complaints	2
E. Bill of Particulars	2
F. Rules for Uniform Traffic Ticket	3
G. Parking Offenses	4
H. Issuing a Traffic Ticket	4
I. Waivers	5
J. Not Guilty Plea by Mail	5
K. Penal Law	5
L. Bicycles	6
M. Local Ordinances	6
N. Non-Resident Drivers	6
O. Vehicles of Non-Residents	6
P. Vehicles Operated for Hire or Profit	6
Q. Reciprocity Laws of Other Places	6
R. Seasonal Farm Laborers	6
S. Military Personnel	7
II. TRAFFIC DIRECTION AND ENFORCEMENT	7
A. Directing Traffic	7
B. Signals	8
C. Pedestrians	8
D. Hazard to Officer	8
E. Tie-Ups	8
F. Capacity Traffic	8
G. Other Considerations	9
H. Questions from the Public	9
I. Alcohol	9
III. ACCIDENTS AND PREVENTION	9
A. Police Reports	9
B. Prevention	9
C. Enforcement Index	10

VEHICLE AND TRAFFIC LAW [V&T]

I. PROVISIONS

Traffic is perhaps the biggest single operation of law enforcement. Intelligent and efficient regulation and control of motor vehicle traffic is one of the major responsibilities of every police department.

The Department of Motor Vehicles publishes annually, as soon as possible after the Legislature adjourns, the complete text of the Vehicle and Traffic Law, and a driver's manual. These publications may be obtained from any office of that department. Every officer should have copies of them for careful study and ready reference.

Officers should also obtain from the Department of Motor Vehicles its "Motor Vehicle Handbook for Patrolmen" and its "Police Accident Report Manual."

The Vehicle and Traffic Law, in Article 1, Sections 100-159, sets forth definitions generally applicable to all traffic laws. Officers should familiarize themselves with these definitions.

A. TRAFFIC INFRACTIONS. - Violation of any provision of the Vehicle and Traffic Law or of any law, ordinance, order, rule or regulation regulating traffic is a traffic infraction if the offense is not declared to be a misdemeanor or felony. A traffic infraction is not a crime. For court and arrest purposes, traffic infractions are handlerd like misdemeanors, except that there can be no jury trial for a traffic infraction and an offender may waive court appearance and ask for disposal of the case by mail in traffic infraction cases (V&T Sec. 155).

B. ABANDONED VEHICLES. - No person may lawfully cause any vehicle to be an abandoned vehicle (V&T Sec. 1224, subd. 6). 1. A motor vehicle is deemed to be an abandoned vehicle if left unattended:

1. With no number plates affixed thereto, for more than six hours on any highway or other public place;
2. For more than twenty-four hours on any highway or other public place, except a portion of a highway or public place on which parking is legally permitted;
3. For more than forty-eight hours, after the parking of such vehicle shall have become illegal, if left on a portion of a highway or public place on which parking is legally permitted;
4. For more than seven days on property of another if left without permission of the owner (V&T Sec. 1224, subd. 1).

If an abandoned vehicle is of a wholesale value in excess of one hundred dollars, the municipality or authority having jurisdiction must make an inquiry concerning the last registered owner and inform that owner of the recovery and disposition requirements according to law (V&T Sec. 1224, subd. 3). If the wholesale value of the abandoned vehicle is less than one hundred dollars, Section 1224, subdivision 2 of the Vehicle and Traffic Law, provides that title to it rests in the municipality or authority.

No person other than one authorized by the appropriate local authority may destroy, deface or remove any part of a vehicle which is left unattended on a highway or other public place without number plates affixed or which is abandoned. An offense under this subdivision is a Class A misdemeanor (V&T Sec. 1224, subd. 7).

C. ARRESTS AND TRAFFIC TICKETS. - For purposes of arrest without, warrant, a traffic infraction may be handled the same as a misdemeanor. Any officer may, without a warrant, arrest and take into custody a driver who has committed a traffic infraction in his presence (V&T Sec. 155).

An officer may issue a Uniform Traffic Ticket in any case of a Vehicle and Traffic Law infraction. Merely issuing a ticket for driving while intoxicated or felony offenses is not recommended. The dangers from merely issuing a traffic ticket and not making a physical arrest ill driving while intoxicated cases are obvious.

It is advisable, for statistical and record purposes, to always issue a Uniform Traffic Ticket in traffic cases, even though a physical arrest is actually made and the defendant is immediately arraigned. This will assist in proper record keeping in connection with convictions of individual operators and chauffeurs.

The Vehicle and Traffic Law gives peace officers additional arrest authority, in that they may, without a warrant, arrest a motor vehicle or motorcycle operator who left the scene of any accident without stopping and giving his name, street address and license number and exhibiting his license to the injured party, or a police officer, or to the nearest police station or judicial officer, where the operator knew that damage was caused to the real or personal property (other than animals) of another, or that personal injury was caused to anyone, or where the vehicle struck and injured any horse, dog or animal classified as cattle (V&T Secs. 600, 601, 602). In order to make such arrest legal the failure to comply must have in fact been committed and the officer must have reasonable cause to believe the Class A misdemeanor (Violation, when involving animals only) was committed by the person arrested (V&T Sec. 602).

Police officers, may, without a warrant, arrest a person for operating a motor vehicle or motorcycle while in an intoxicated condition or while ability to operate is impaired by alcohol, even if the offense was not in their presence. The offense must in fact have been committed and must involve an accident or collision and the officer must have reasonable cause to believe that the offense was committed by the person arrested (V&T Sec. 1193).

An officer issuing a Uniform Traffic Ticket may do so either on personal knowledge or upon information and belief (Peo. vs. Tennyson, 19 N.Y. 2d. 573). The Uniform Traffic Ticket is not a criminal summons or court summons, but is merely an invitation to the defendant to appear in court at the time and place designated. It gives the court no jurisdiction until the defendant appears and no penalty attaches for failure to heed it (Coville vs. Bennett, 57 Misc. 2d. 838).

D. TRAFFIC INFORMATION OR COMPLAINTS. - The Part II copy of a Uniform Traffic Ticket is ordinarily used by officers as their complaint or information, to charge the traffic offender. This is referred to as a "simplified traffic information" (CCP Sec. 147-a, 147-g). A regular information or complaint form may, of course, be used in any traffic case, whenever desired by the officer.

Whether the officer's simplified (or other) traffic information is based on his personal knowledge or upon information and belief (i,e., upon data from an informant or other person), it is sufficient in itself, without added details or supporting affidavits or depositions, to give the court jurisdiction. But if the defendant will not appear and it is necessary that a warrant be issued for his arrest, the officer, to secure the warrant, must furnish the court sufficient probable cause to issue the warrant, He must do so in the form of affidavit or testimony under oath (Peo. vs, Boback, 23 N.Y, 2d, 189).

E. BILL OF PARTICULARS. - The amount of Information set forth in any simplified traffic information is, of course, very limited. Therefore, on the arraignment of the defendant or at any later time, the court must inform the defendant of his right to a bill of particulars, and if the defendant requests, must direct the arresting officer to file a bill of particulars (CCP Sec. 147-f).

No special form is required for a bill of particulars, but it must be either affirmed under penalty of perjury or sworn. The officer must either sign it and indicate in it that he affirms its information under penalty of perjury, or he must swear to it before an authorized person. The bill must have the following in it:

1. Title of the action Cspecify name of court, show "People of the State of New York" as plaintiffs and show full name of defendant or defendants).
2. A statement in ordinary language of such particulars as may be necessary to give the defendant and the court reasonable information as to the nature and character of the offense charged.
   a. The statute specifies that it is not necessary to set out items of evidence in any bill of particulars nor is it necessary to set forth all the elements of the offense (CCP Sec. 147-g, subd. 1, 2).

F. RULES FOR UNIFORM TRAFFIC TICKET. - Officers issuing a ticket instead of making a physical arrest for a traffic offense (except parking) must use a Uniform Traffic Ticket conforming to Regulations of the Commissioner of Motor Vehicles (V&T Sec. 207, subd. 1; Regulations of the Commissioner, Sec. 94.2). New York City is excepted from this requirement and officers there may use tickets conforming to local ordinance (V&T Sec. 207, subd. 4).

The chief executive officer of each law enforcement agency is required by law to provide all records and reports on Uniform Traffic Tickets required by the Commissioner of Motor Vehicles (V&T Sec. 207, subd. 2).

Tickets must be in the form prescribed by the Commissioner and must have serial numbers of not over six digits (Regulations of the Commissioner, Sec. 91.5 91.6). The tickets must be in at least five parts, with interleaved carbons (Regulations of the Commissioner, Sec. 91.5).

Law enforcement agencies must procure tickets at their own expense (Regulations of the Commissioner, Sec. 91.9).

At the expiration of one month from the end of each calendar quarter of the year, every law enforcement agency must report to the Commissioner on all Uniform Traffic Tickets issued by its officers, showing:

1. Packets of tickets assigned;
2. Tickets issued by officers;
3. Tickets disposed of and disposition;
4. Tickets still pending;
5. Voided, mutilated, or destroyed tickets or packets.

The report must be submitted within 45 days of the end of the quarter (Regulations of the Commissioner, Sec. 91.10).

Any officer losing a ticket or packet of tickets must prepare an official report for his law enforcement agency.

Law enforcement agencies must retain a duplicate copy of their quarterly reports and must retain for at least 2 years the enforcement agency's copy of every Uniform Traffic Ticket issued (Regulations of the Commissioner, Sec. 91.10, subd. d, e, f).

The duplicate copy of the summons (Part two) retained by the officer is the simplified traffic information. The officer must sign and swear to it before the magistrate or any chief, deputy chief, captain, lieutenant or acting lieutenant, or sergeant or acting sergeant, of a police department, or any sheriff, undersheriff, chief deputy, deputy sergeant or deputy in charge of any road patrol maintained by any sheriff in the county to whom the officer reports service of the ticket (Regulations of the Commissioner, Sec. 91.11; V&T Sec. 208). The officer may, instead of swearing, affirm under penalty of perjury. The officer must deliver to the court Parts 2, 3, and 4 of the Uniform Traffic Ticket and must keep Part 5 (Regulations of the Commissioner, Sec. 91.11).

Any person who disposes of any uniform traffic summons and complaint in any manner other than that prescribed by law, is guilty of a Class A misdemeanor (V&T Sec. 207, subd. 5).

G. PARKING OFFENSES. - A Uniform Traffic Ticket cannot be used for parking offenses. A "parking ticket" must be used. These are not covered by the Commissioner's regulations and each department may devise its own. They are always issued in the name of the owner of the motor vehicle (using the vehicle's license number). They are ordinarily merely left under the windshield wiper or tied to a door handle or radio aerial, in the absence of the operator. If the operator is known, the ticket may be issued personally to him. It is presumed that a parked motor vehicle with no operator present was parked by its owner. The presumption may be rebutted in court by the owner offering proof that another operator parked it (Peo. vs. Rubin, 284 N.Y. 392). This presumption does not apply to any other kind of traffic case (Peo. vs. Hildebrandt, 308 N.Y. 397).

H. ISSUING A TRAFFIC TICKET. - Once the safety and emergency precautions for properly stopping and approaching a pursued vehicle have been properly carried out, the officer may then proceed to act on the traffic offense, if one exists. He should politely request the operator to produce his driver's license and the registration for the vehicle. The operator should then be advised of the specific offense and the ticket issued forthwith (one ticket for each traffic offense).

The officer should avoid any unnecessary conversation while issuing the traffic ticket. He should be firm but pleasant and courteous, and he should offer no excuse for the issuance of any ticket. If the offense is one of a grade less than a misdemeanor the officer may wish to call the violator's attention to procedures for pleas by mail. When the offense is one of lighting defects (except where both headlights are defective: V&T Sec. 376-a, subd. 2),the officer should advise the violator of the "acceptable proof of repair or adjustment" procedure in Sec. 376-a, subd. 4 of the Vehicle and Traffic Law. (Complaint must be dismissed if offender returns next day with proof of repair and compliance.)

Weather permitting, the officer should stand outside his patrol car while completing the ticket summons. Before proceeding to his patrol car he should instruct the operator and other occupants of the pursued vehicle that they must remain in their vehicle for safety reasons. If, during the ticket issuing, any of the occupants leave the stopped vehicle, the officer should cease writing and direct his attention to them to prevent accident, injury or any unusual incident.

After dark (and during inclement weather), the officer will necessarily need to execute the ticket in his patrol car. Situations of this sort will not present a particular problem if the stopped vehicle is in proper position with the headlights of the patrol car illuminating the stopped vehicle. It is recommended that the operator being ticketed not be permitted in the patrol car while a ticket is being issued. Tickets for later appearance may be issued to any resident of New York State or of any State with which New Tork has established a Violators Compact (Connecticut, Massachusetts, Rhode Island, Vermont, and New Jersey).

Good judgment should be exercised in the issuance of a traffic ticket. If there is an indication or reason to suspect that the violator will not appear in compliance with a ticket, he should be arrested and arraigned immediately, or released on bail. If the violator is to be immediately arraigned, he must be told that he is under arrest and should be handled with all due caution as an arrested person.

When writing a ticket, use a ball-point pen to insure legibility of all copies. Print all information in block letters (except officer's affirmation of complaint on the second copy, which should be separately signed and dated by the issuing officer). Erasures are not acceptable. If a mistake is made, draw a single line through the error and print the correct information above. If the mistake is of such a nature that it would be impractical to correct, issue another ticket to the violator. Officers must be familiar with the procedures of their department for "voiding" tickets.

Record the violator's name on the ticket exactly as it appears on the driver's license. Fill in all other blocks pertaining to the violator, his license and the vehicle being operated. If the State issuing the license differs from the violator's State of residence, enter the abbreviation of the name of the State of issuance in the box marked "Type of License" along with the type of license. Check the appropriate box (Village-Town-City or District) to designate the court before which the defendant is to appear, and fill in the blanks identifying the jurisdiction (Town or City, etc.,of ......). Record the location of the court with the complete mailing address. Write in the "Day of the Week" upon which the offense occurred. If the offense involves the Vehicle and Traffic Law, the word "or" must be crossed out. If the offense is another law, cross out the "NYS V&T Law" and on the following line show the proper title of the law violated.

Use the list of offenses as published in the "Abridged Names of Violations of the Vehicle and Traffic Law" in the "Motor Vehicle Handbook for Patrolmen."

I. WAIVERS. - Traffic infractions may be disposed of without the personal appearance of the defendant for the purpose of entering a plea of guilty, except in the following cases:
    1. Third of subsequent speeding offense within 18 months
    2. Any offense in New York City
    3. Any misdemeanor or felony

The application must be in the form of an affidavit and must be accompanied by the "record of conviction" stub of the violator's license. The form of affidavit must be exactly as prescribed by the Commissioner of Motor Vehicles and every officer issuing a ticket to a violator must hand the violator a copy of the form, to use if he chooses (CCP Sec. 335, subd. 2).

The form prescribed is set out in Regulations of the Commissioner, Section 92.2. It may be printed on the back of Part 1 of the Uniform Traffic Ticket (Regulations of the Commissioner, Sec. 91.7, subd. a-3). This is the usual and most convenient way to furnish the form and ensures that the officer will not omit the statutory duty to furnish it when he issues a ticket.

J. NOT GUILTY PLEA BY MAIL. - In addition to appearing personally to enter a plea of not guilty to a traffic infraction (Vehicle and Traffic Law or any local law, ordinance, order, rule or regulation relating to the operation of motor vehicle or motorcycles), a defendant may enter a plea of not guilty by mailing to the court the ticket making the charge and a signed statement indicating such plea. The plea must be sent by registered or certified mail, return receipt requested, within forty-eight hours after receiving the ticket. Upon receipt of the ticket and statement, the court must advise the violator Cby registered or certified mail) of a trial date, not less than seven days after the notice of trial is mailed (CCP Sec. 335-b; V&T Sec. 1800, subd. e).

K. PENAL LAW. - Vehicle offenses of concern to all officers are found not only in the Vehicle and Traffic Law but also in the Penal Law:
    1. *Criminally Negligent Homicide.* - A person commits Criminally Negligent Homicide when, with criminal negligence, he causes the death of another (P.L. Sec. 125-10).
    2. *Manslaughter.* - A person commits Manslaughter Second when he recklessly causes the death of another person (P.L. Sec. 125.15).
    3. *Menacing.* - A person commits Menacing when, by physical menace, he intentionally places or attempts to place another person in fear of imminent serious physical injury (e.g., teenagers playing "chicken" with cars) (P.L. Sec. 120.15).

4. Reckless Endangerment. - A person is guilty of Reckless Endangerment Second who recklessly engages in conduct which creates a substantial risk of serious physical injury to another (P.L. Sec. 120.20).

5. Assault. - A person commits Assault Third when he recklessly causes physical injury to another (P.L. Sec. 120.00).

L. *BICYCLES.* - Sections 1230 through 1236 of the Vehicle and Traffic Law cover the use of bicycles on the highway. Section 1231 makes the traffic rights and duties applicable to drivers of vehicles also applicable to riders of bicycles, subject to the special regulations in Sections 1230 and 1232-1236.

M. *LOCAL ORDINANCES.* - Articles 38, 39 and 40 of the Vehicle and Traffic Law permit additional regulation of traffic by public authorities and commissions, by cities and villages and by the County Superintendent of Roads in counties. Officers must familiarize themselves with their pertinent local ordinances and rules and regulations of authorities and commissions on highways within the officer's jurisdiction.

N. *NON-RESIDENT DRIVERS.* - No person under age 16 may operate a motor vehicle in New York on an out-of-state license. A person age 16 or over, but under the age of 18, is permitted to operate a motor vehicle on an out-of-state license but under the same restrictions imposed on a New York junior operator license under Vehicle and Traffic Law Section 501, subd. b (V&T sec. 250, subd. 2).

Persons 18 and over who are non-residents and from a state, territory, federal district or foreign country whose laws do require licensing to operate a motor vehicle or motorcycle, may drive in New York on the out-of-state license. They may drive their own, their families' or any other vehicle. This driving privilege is reciprocal - it operates only to the extent that the other jurisdiction grants driving privileges to New York drivers (V&T Sec. 250, subd. 2). If the non-resident becomes a New York resident, he can drive on his out-of-state license for 60 days pending obtaining a New York license (V&T Sec. 250, subd. 2).

O. *VEHICLES OF NON-RESIDENTS.* - Motor vehicles, motorcycles and trailers owned by non-residents of the state may be operated in New York if they are duly registered and equipped and display registration numbers as required by the laws of the owner's place of residence. This privilege, like the licensing privilege, is reciprocal and operates only to the extent that the owner's place of residence gives operating privileges to New York-owned vehicles (V&T Sec. 250, subd.1).

P. *VEHICLES OPERATED FOR HIRE OR PROFIT.* - Out-of-state registered vehicles engaged in transporting persons or property for hire or profit from point-to-point within New York have no privilege at all and may not lawfully operate in New York, except the following:

1. An out-of-state registered semi-trailer drawn by a tractor registered in New York.
2. An out-of-state registered trailer drawn by a motor vehicle registered and owned in New York, provided no property is both placed upon and unloaded from the trailer within New York.
3. An out-of-state registered vehicle cannot be used on any work under contract for a public improvement for the state, a municipality, a school district or a commission appointed by law, except that it may transport machinery, tools or plant equipment to perform the contract (V&T Sec. 250, subd. 3).

Q. *RECIPROCITY LAWS OF OTHER PLACES.* - Officers should obtain from the Department of Motor Vehicles a copy of its publication "State of New York Motor Vehicle Reciprocity Summary" in order to be informed of the specific privileges of non-resident drivers from the different states in the United States and from other countries.

R. *SEASONAL FARM LABORERS.* - Between April 1 and November 30 annually, non-resident seasonal farm laborers are permitted to drive on license and registration of their own place of residence, but must file proof with the Commissioner of Motor Vehicles that they are insured and receive from the Commissioner a certificate (for the vehicle) which must be affixed to a prominent place in the interior of the vehicle and/or a personal driving permit (V&T Sec. 250, subd. 4-a). Such laborers have 30 days from the date of entry into New York to procure the certificate and/or permit (V&T Sec. 250, subd. 4-d). The fee for certificate or permit is $2.00.

S. MILITARY PERSONNEL. - Motor vehicles or motorcycles having registrations and displaying plates issued by the armed forces of the United States for vehicles owned by members of the armed forces or their dependents are exempt from New York registration for a period of 45 days after the owner enters New York to either travel to his residence or a point of military duty (V&T Sec. 251).

A New York operator's license of a person entering the armed forces expires on the 30th of September following either the expiration date of the Defense Emergency Act (7/1/68) or 60 days after a person is separated from the service, whichever is first (Unconsol. Laws, Sec. 9196, subd. 3).

A New York chauffeur's license of a person entering the armed forces expires on the 31st of May following either the expiration of the Defense Emergency Act (7/1/68) or 60 days after the person is separated from the service, whichever is first (Unconsol. Laws, Sec. 9196, subd. 3).

If the person entered the armed forces on or after 7/1/63, the advantages in the previous two paragraphs may be secured only if the person notified the Commissioner of Motor Vehicles of his entry into service, as required by Section 501, subdivision 1, paragraph g of the Vehicle and Traffic Law (Unconsol. Law, Sec. 9196, subd. 3).

Members of the armed forces or their dependents who are nonresidents of this state may operate a motor vehicle or trailer in New York provided the registration, equipment and display of registration numbers of the vehicle are as required by law in the state of his residence (V&T Sec. 251, subd. 3).

Any member of the armed forces who has been issued a motor vehicle or motorcycle operator's license by the armed forces can operate non-official (i.e., not armed forces on official business) motor vehicles or motorcycles on it on New York highways only for a period of 60 days after entering New York (V&T Sec. 251).

II. TRAFFIC DIRECTION AND ENFORCEMENT

The purpose of traffic direction is to give the users of streets and highways the greatest freedom of movement consistent with safety and the rights of others.

The traffic officer's contact with the public is much more frequent than that of any other officer. For many people, their only contact with police agencies or law enforcement officers is with traffic officers. The public may thus judge a department solely on the appearance and ability of its traffic officers. The traffic officer is frequently subjected to tests of self-control. In spite of this, he must maintain an aggreeable attitude and control his temper. Performance of his duty in a firm but courteous manner will creat confidence in his ability and in his department.

A. DIRECTING TRAFFIC. - Successful traffic direction depends upon continued analysis by the officer of the changing needs of his post and upon giving correct instructions to drivers and pedestrians. When directing traffic, the officer must be certain that:

    1. The instruction is necessary
    2. The instruction can be executed
    3. The instruction is clear and can be easily understood

4. The instruction can be and is promptly withdrawn when it has served its purpose

The traffic officer's instructions are ordinarily given by hand-and-arm and whistle signals. The purpose of the signals is to let drivers and pedestrians know what the officer wants them to do. The traffic officer's ability is measured by the response of drivers and pedestrians to his instructions and by the prompt and safe movement of traffic.

B. SIGNALS - Hand-and-arm signals should be given at or above shoulder height for best visibility. A whistle should not be used as a means of giving signals but merely as an auxiliary to the hand-and-arm signals. It should be blown as a warning or preparatory command, the actual direction being given by the hand-and-arm signal. Good, usable signals are:

1. To stop vehicle approaching from the right, turn head to right, raise right arm to shoulder height with the index finger pointed toward the vehicle. Look directly at the driver and try to get his attention.
2. To start vehicles on the right, turn head to right, raise right arm to shoulder height with the index finger pointed toward the driver. Hold arm rigid from shoulder to elbow, bend the arm at the elbow and bring the hand down in a circular movement in front of the face.
3. Traffic on the left of the officer should be handled as in 1 and 2, using left in place of right.
4. In handling left turns, direct the turning car so that it is close to the officer, in the center of the highway. It is then in a position to complete the turn at the first opportunity. Traffic officers should encourage a short left turn in front of the officer. This permits two vehicles to be moved at the same time without interference with each other. It is preferable to a long turn around the officer, from a standpoint of both time and safety.

In changing direction of traffic flow, do not wait for stragglers. To do so results in loss of time. Move accumulated vehicles which are at a standstill and waiting. When stragglers are reached, change the direction of traffic flow. In the interval, stragglers will accumulate and be ready for the next change. The officer should regulate the time of changing traffic so as to safely move the greatest number of vehicles and still keep none waiting for unreasonable lengths of time. Never give a signal to start or stop without looking in all directions affected to make sure that compliance with the signal will not result in an accident.

C. PEDESTRIANS. - When directing pedestrian traffic, an officer may signal "stop" by raising both arms to a position horizontal with the shoulders, palms facing the pedestrians and release the pedestrians by swinging the arms in a circular movement across the chest.

D. HAZARD TO OFFICER. - The position of an officer directing traffic at a busy intersection is one of great personal danger. This hazard is somewhat reduced by making an effort to educate the motoring public never to pass a traffic officer when he is facing them or has his back toward them, but to wait until they may pass in a line parallel with his chest or back, at which time he is in a position to observe moving traffic approaching from his right and left.

E. TIE-UPS. - In the event of a traffic tie-up, the situation is like an arch held in place by a keystone. Find the keystone (a car stalled, mechanical trouble, accident, attempt to turn against traffic), and remove it. In the event of congestion, arrange to divert traffic through parallel streets, making sure that traffic is diverted into streets having outlets and not into dead ends.

F. CAPACITY TRAFFIC. - Every street and highway has a maximum capacity or saturation point. When this point is reached, traffic becomes an engineering problem. The officer can improve the situation only by remaining calm, even in the face of irritating remarks, blowing horns, etc. He must attempt to keep as many vehicles moving as possible. In handling traffic congestion, the officer must remember not to become excited. When emotion of any kind takes over, a person loses his ability to think clearly or reason logically. The officer's job is to remove excitement, not to add to it.

G. OTHER CONSIDERATIONS. - If it is necessary for an officer to talk with a driver or to issue a summons, he must avoid blocking traffic. The driver must be directed to drive to the side of the road before stopping. When giving a summons, all unnecessary talk must be avoided. The officer should be brief and businesslike.

In addition to handling traffic, the traffic officer is in a position to make important arrests. Alarms should be studied care-fully. The automobile is used by most criminals. While on traffic post, the officer has an excellent opportunity to observe people who are wanted.

H. QUESTIONS FROM THE PUBLIC. - Many people regularly ask traffic officers questions regarding routes, points of interest, etc. Furnishing information of this kind is recognized as an important police service. Officers should familiarize themselves with such information to quickly and intelligently answer inquiries. Proper handling of on-the-street inquiries is a major factor in good public relations.

I. ALCOHOL. - Officers should review sections covering "Intoxication" and "Laboratory Examinations," for information pertaining to driving while intoxicated or driving while ability impaired cases.

III. ACCIDENTS AND PREVENTION

A. POLICE REPORTS. - Whenever an accident involving personal injury is reported to an officer he must immediately investigate the facts or cause them to be investigated and report the results to the Commissioner of Motor Vehicles forthwith (V&T Sec, 603). No investigation is required by the law if the report of the accident is not made to the officer within five days after such accident. Individual departments may adopt rules to require reporting in such instances if they choose to do so.

B. PREVENTION. - There are three principal methods of preventing traffic accidents: Engineering, Education, and Enforcement.

Enforcement is the direct responsibility of the law enforcement officer. It is a quick and direct means of obtaining results when intelligently applied in sufficient quantity.

When traffic enforcement is adequate, accidents caused by law violations are reduced and motorists learn respect for the law. A strong deterrent results from efficient and constant patrolling and strict enforcement.

In order to be most effective, enforcement activities must be carefully planned and selective - they must be directed to the area where they can accomplish the most in preventing accidents rather than be applied without plan, or hazhazardly.

To do this requires planning based on adequate statistics concerning accidents and accident locations.

Ineffective traffic law enforcement permits the accident rate to remain static or increase. The public attitude toward the police and traffic laws will be undesirable in such circumstances.

The police administrator can determine, from study of accident statistics, when and where to assign traffic patrols, what offenses are contributing to accidents, and which should be given major enforcement attention. This is "Selective Enforcement."

Most accidents are caused by traffic infractions. In order for the police to determine which offenses are contributing to accidents in any one municipality or area, it is necessary to study accident records and reports for that particular location. Before accident records can be relied upon to procure accurate, usable data, an investigation must be made of each accident. Officers must be trained to investigate accidents and to prepare reports containing such descriptions of accidents that those who read and analyze the reports can construct each accident, prepare a collision diagram, and tally the infraction or infractions which contributed to the accident, by type, time and location.

An accident spot-map will show at a glance on which highway or s street and in which areas accidents most frequently occur. A review of the accident records for that highway, street, or area will show the time the accidents are occurring, and which offenses are contributing factors. This will permit directing special attention to high-accident locations, with patrols at specific times alert for the accident-producing offenses. A comparison should be made of the times of day traffic arrests are being made on high-accident highways and the times of day accidents are occurring there. If there is a significant discrepancy in times, adjustments must be made so that times of enforcement activities and accident experience will closely coincide. A comparison should also be made between the accident-produeing causes and arrests, and, if there is a significant difference between the two, adjustments in enforcement activity must be made.

C. ENFORCEMENT INDEX. - The Enforcement Index of any area is the ratio of the number of fatal and personal injury accidents in the area to the number of convictions with penalty for Hazardous Moving Offenses in the area (speeding, reckless driving, failing to keep right, changing lanes unsafely, passing a red light or stop sign, and most other traffic infractions committed while the vehicle is moving). Only penalties such as fines or jail sentences are counted. Arrests resulting in suspended judgment or sentence or in dismissal are not considered when computing the index.

The Enforcement Index is a useful method of measuring the effect of enforcement activities on the accident rate in an area, municipality, or on a specific highway. The index also measures the quantity and quality of traffic arrests. Police administrators can determine from it whether officers should make more arrests per accident, whether more men are needed in an area, or whether arrests are or are not being made for accident-producing offenses.

There is a wide range in enforcement indices in various area. Some jurisdictions with a low traffic accident rate have found an Enforcement Index of 5 produced good results. Others have found it necessary to go as high as 15 or 20.

A usual procedure is to increase the amount of enforcement until a further increase fails to produce a corresponding drop in accidents. This is assumed to be the point of diminishing returns beyond which additional enforcement becomes an inefficient method of accident prevention.

A low index points up a necessity for more convictions with penalty for moving hazardous offenses. This can be accomplished by placing more patrols in the area or by instructing officers in the area to increase the quality and quantity of their enforcement activities. It may also indicate that too many arrests are being closed by the courts without a penalty.

When only a limited number of officers are available to patrol a high-accident location, or when the work-time of such officers is divided between traffic and general police duties, and a low Enforcement Index results, it is clearly evident that additional officers are required in order to produce a reduction in offenses and accidents.

If a high Enforcement Index is obtained in an area without a significant reduction in accidents, it is evident that the point of diminishing return has been reached. Enforcement efforts should not be reduced. Such a situation indicates that accidents are being caused by factors other than infractions, such as highway grades, alignment, inadequate traffic control devices, or drivers skidding, falling asleep or being inattentive, etc., and steps other than on-the-road enforcement are required.

GLOSSARY OF TRAFFIC CONTROL TERMS

TABLE OF CONTENTS

	Page
Access Road ... Desire Line	1
Divided Street ... Left Turn Lane	2
Manual Traffic Control ... Passenger Vehicle	3
Passenger (Transit) Volume ... Separate Turning Lane	4
Shoulder ... Traffic Accident	5
Traffic Actuated Controller ... Uninterrupted Flow	6
Vehicle ... Zone (Origin-Destination Studies)	7

GLOSSARY OF TRAFFIC CONTROL TERMS

A

ACCESS ROAD - Public roads, existing or proposed, needed to provide essential access to military installation and facilities, or to industrial installations and facilities in the activities of which there is specific defense interest. Roads within the boundaries of military reservation are excluded from this definition unless such roads have been dedicated to public use and are not subject to closure.

ACCIDENT SPOT MAP - An area or installation map showing the location of vehicle accidents by means of symbols. Symbols may represent accidents classified as to daylight hours, night hours, injury or death.

ANGLE PARKING - Parking where the longitudinal axes of vehicles form an angle with the alignment of the roadway.

C

CENTER LINE - A line marking the center of a roadway between traffic moving in opposite direction.

COLLISION DIAGRAM - A plan of an intersection or section of roadway on which reported accidents are diagramed by means of arrows showing manner of collision.

COMBINED CONDITION AND COLLISION DIAGRAM - A condition diagram upon which the reported accidents are diagramed by means of arrows showing manner of collision.

CONDITION DIAGRAM - A plan of an intersection or section of roadway showing all objects and physical conditions having a bearing on traffic movement and safety at that location. Usually these are scaled drawings.

CORDON COUNTS - A count of all vehicles and persons entering and leaving a district (cordon area) during a designated period of time.

CORDON AREA - The district bounded by the cordon line and included in a cordon count.

CROSSWALK - Any portion of a roadway at an intersection or elsewhere distinctly indicated for pedestrian crossing by lines or other markings on the surface. Also, that part of a roadway at an intersection included within the connections of the lateral lines of the sidewalks on opposite sides of the traffic way measured from the curbs, or in the absence of curbs, from the edges of the traversable roadway.

D

DELAY - The time consumed while traffic or a specified component of traffic is impeded in its movement by some element over which it has no control usually expressed in seconds per vehicle.

DESIRE LINE - A straight line between the point of origin and point of destination of a trip without regard to routes of travel (used in connection with an origin-destination study).

DIVIDED STREET - A two-way road on which traffic in one direction of travel is separated from that in the opposite direction by a directional separator. Such a road has two or more roadways.

E

85 PERCENTILE SPEED - That speed below which 85 percent of the traffic unit's travel, and above which 15 percent travel.

F

FIXED-TIME CONTROLLER - An automatic controller for supervising the operation of traffic control signals in accordance with a predetermined fixed time cycle and divisions thereof.

FIXED-TIME TRAFFIC SIGNAL - A traffic signal operated by a fixed-time controller.

FLASHING BEACON - A section of a standard traffic signal head, or a similar type device, having a yellow or red lens in each face, which is illuminated by rapid intermittent flashes.

FLASHING TRAFFIC SIGNAL - A traffic control signal used as a flashing beacon.

FLOATING CAR - An automobile driven in the traffic flow at the average speed of the surrounding vehicles.

FLOW DIAGRAM - The graphical representation of the traffic volumes on a road or street network or section thereof, showing by means of bands the relative volumes using each section of roadway during a given period of time, usually 1 hour.

H

HIGH FREQUENCY ACCIDENT LOCATION - A specific location where a large number of traffic accidents have occurred.

I

INTERSECTION APPROACH - That portion of an intersection leg which is used by traffic approaching the intersection.

L

LATERAL CLEARANCE - The distance between the edge of pavement and any lateral obstruction.

LATERAL OBSTRUCTION - Any fixed object located adjacent to the traveled way which reduces the transverse dimensions of the roadway.

LEFT TURN LANE - A lane within the normal surfaced width reserved for left turning vehicles.

M

MANUAL TRAFFIC CONTROL - The use of-hand signals or manually operated devices by traffic control personnel to control traffic.

MANUAL COUNTER - A tallying device which is operated by hand.

MASS TRANSPORTATION - Movement of large groups of persons.

MULTIAXLE TRUCK - A truck which has more than two axles.

O

OCCUPANCY RATIO -The average number-of occupants per vehicle (including the driver).

ODOMETER -A device on a vehicle for measuring the distance traveled, usually as a cumulative total, but sometimes also for individual trips, with an indicator on the instrument panel where it is usually combined with a speedometer indicator, or in the hub of a wheel in some trucks.

OFF-PEAK PERIOD - That portion of the day in which traffic volumes are relatively light.

OFFSET LANES - Additional lanes used for traffic which is heavier in one direction. Also known as unbalanced lanes.

OFF-STREET PARKING - Lots and garages intended for parking entirely off streets and alleys. street and alleys (may be angle or parallel parking) for parking of vehicles.

ORIGIN DESTINATION STUDIES - A study of the origins and destinations of trips of vehicles and passengers. Usually included in the study are all trips within, or passing through, into or out of a selected area.

OVERALL SPEED - The total distance traversed divided by the travel time. Usually expressed in miles per hour and includes all delays.

OVERALL TIME - The time of travel, including stops and delays except those off the traveled way.

P

PARALLEL PARKING - Parking where the longitudinal axis of vehicles are parallel to alignment of the roadway so that the vehicles are facing in the same direction as the movement of adjacent vehicular traffic.

PARKING DURATION - Length of time a vehicle is parked.

PASSENGER VEHICLE - A free-wheeled, self-propelled vehicle designed for the transportation of persons but limited in seating capacity to not more than seven passengers, not including the driver. It includes taxicabs, limousines, and station wagons, but does not include motorcycles.
(In capacity studies, also includes light reconnaissance vehicles, and pickup trucks.)

PASSENGER (TRANSIT) VOLUME - The total number of public transit occupants being transported in a period of time.

PEAK PERIOD - That portion of the day in which maximum traffic volumes are experienced.

PEDESTRIAN - Any person afoot. For purpose of accident classification, this will be interpreted to include any person riding in or upon a device moved or designed for movement by human power or the force of gravity, except bicycles, including stilts, skates, skis, sleds, toy wagons, and scooters.

PERCENT OF GRADE - The slope in the longitudinal direction of the pavement expressed in percent which is the number of units of change in elevation per 100 units of horizontal distance.

PERCENT OF GREEN TIME - The percentage of green time allotted to the direction of travel being studies.

PROPERTY DAMAGE - Damage to property as a result of a motor vehicle accident that may be a basis of a claim for compensation. Does not include compensation for loss of life or for personal injuries.

PUBLIC HIGHWAYS- The entire width between property lines, or boundary lines, of every way or place of which any part is open to use of the public for purposes of vehicular traffic as a matter of right or custom.

PUBLIC TRANSIT - The public passenger carryi ng service afforded by vehicles following regular routes and making specified stops.

R

REFLECTORIZE - The application of some material to traffic control devices or hazards which will return to the eyes of the road user some portion of the light from his vehicle headlights, thereby producing a brightness which attracts attention.

REGULATORY DEVICE - A device used to indicate the required method of traffic movement or use of the public traffic way.

REGULATORY SIGN - A sign used to indicate the required method of traffic movement or use of the traffic way.

RIGHT TURN LANE - A lane within the normal surfaced width reserved for right turning vehicles.

ROADWAY - That portion of a traffic way including shoulders, improved, designed, or ordinarily used for vehicle traffic.

S

SEPARATE TURNING LANE - Added traffic lane which is separated from the intersection area by an island or unpaved area. It may be wide enough for one or two line operation

SHOULDER - The portion of the roadway contiguous with the traveled way for accommodation of stopped vehicles, for emergency use, and for lateral support of base and surface courses.

SIGHT DISTANCES - The length of roadway visible to the driver of a passenger vehicle at any given point on the roadway when the view is unobstructed by traffic.

SIGNAL CYCLE - The total time required for one complete sequence of the intervals of a traffic signal.

SIGNAL CONTROLLER - A complete electrical mechanism for controlling the operation of traffic control signals, including the timer and all necessary auxiliary apparatus mounted in a cabinet.

SIGNAL FACE - That part of a signal head provided for controlling traffic from a single direction.

SIGNAL HEAD - An assembly containing one or more signal faces that may be designated accordingly as one-way, two-way, multi-way.

SIGNAL PHASE - A part of the total time cycle allocated to movements receiving the right-of-way or to any combination ments receiving the right-of-way simultaneously during one

SIMPLE INTERSECTION - An intersection of two traffic ways, approaches.

SPEED - The rate of movement of a vehicle, generally expressed in miles per hour.

STOPPING SIGHT DISTANCE – The distance required by a drive of a vehicle, given speed, to bring vehicle to a stop after and object becomes visible.

STREET WIDTH - The width of the paved or traveled portion of the roadway.

T

THROUGH MOVEMENT - (See THROUGH TRAFFIC)

THROUGH STREET - A street on which traffic is given the right-of-way so that vehicles entering or crossing the street must yield the right-of-way.

THROUGH TRAFFIC - Traffic proceeding through a military installation or portion not originating in or destined to that military installation or portion thereof.

TIME CYCLE - (See SIGNAL CYCLE)

TRAFFIC - Pedestrians, ridden or herded animals, vehicles, street cars, and other conveyances, either singly or together, while using any street for purposes of travel.

TRAFFIC ACCIDENT - Any accident involving a motor vehicle in motion that results in death, injury, or property damage.

TRAFFIC ACTUATED CONTROLLER- An automatic controller for supervising the operation of traffic control signals in accordance with the immediate and varying demands of traffic as registered with the-controller by means of detectors.

TRAFFIC CONTROL - All measures except those of a structural kind that serve to control and guide traffic and to promote road safety.

TRAFFIC CONTROL DEVICE - A Traffic control device is any sign, signal, marking, or device placed or erected for the purpose of regulating, warning, or guiding traffic.

TRAFFIC DEMAND - The volume of traffic desiring to use a particular route or facility.

TRAFFIC ENGINEERING - That phase of engineering that deals with the planning and geometric design of streets, highways, and abutting lands, and with traffic operations thereon, as their use is related to the safe, convenient, and economic transportation of persons and goods.

TRAFFIC FLOW - The movement of vehicles on a roadway.

TRAFFIC FLOW PATTERN - The distribution of traffic volumes on a street or highway network~

TRAFFIC GENERATOR - A traffic producing area such as a post exchange, parking lot, or administrative center.

TRAFFIC SIGNAL INTERVAL - Anyone of the several divisions of the total time cycle during which signal indications do not change.

TRAFFICWAY - The entire width between property lines (or other boundary lines) of every way or place of which any part is open to use of public for purposes of vehicular traffic as a matter of right or custom.

TRANSIT VEHICLE - A passenger carrying vehicle, such as a bus or streetcar which follows regular routes and makes specific stops.

TRAVEL TIME- The total elapsed time from the origin to destination of a trip.

TURNING MOVEMENT - The traffic making a designated turn at an intersection.

TWO-WAY STREETS - A street on which traffic may move in opposite directions simultaneously. It may be either divided or undivided.

TYPE OF ACCIDENT - The kind of motor vehicle accident, such as head-on, right-angle, etc.

TYPE OF SURFACE - The class of surface such as concrete, asphalt, gravel, etc.

U

UNINTERRRUPTED FLOW - The flow of-vehicles under ideal conditions resulting in unrestricted movement.

V

VEHICLE - Every device in, upon, or by which any person or property is or may be transported or drawn upon a highway, except those devices moved by human power or used exclusively upon stationary rails or tracks.

VEHICULE OCCUPANCY - The average number of occupants per automobile, including the driver.

VOLUME - The number of vehicles passing a given point during a specified period of time.

W

WARNING SIGN - A sign used to indicate conditions that are actually or potentially hazardous to highway users.

WARRANT - Formally stated conditions that have been accepted as minimum requirements for justifying installation of a traffic control device or regulation.

Z

ZONE (ORIGIN-DESTINATION STUDIES) -- A division of an area established for the purpose of analyzing origin-destination studies. It may be bounded by physical barriers such as rivers and highways, or may be the location of individual work organizations that have duty stations in relatively close proximity.

GLOSSARY OF LEGAL TERMS

TABLE OF CONTENTS

	Page
Action ... Affiant	1
Affidavit ... At Bar	2
At Issue ... Burden of Proof	3
Business ... Commute	4
Complainant ... Conviction	5
Cooperative ... Demur (v.)	6
Demurrage ... Endorsement	7
Enjoin ... Facsimile	8
Factor ... Guilty	9
Habeas Corpus ... Incumbrance	10
Indemnify ... Laches	11
Landlord and Tenant ... Malice	12
Mandamus ... Obiter Dictum	13
Object (v.) ... Perjury	14
Perpetuity ... Proclamation	15
Proffered Evidence ... Referee	16
Referendum ... Stare Decisis	17
State ... Term	18
Testamentary ... Warrant (Warranty) (v.)	19
Warrant (n.) ... Zoning	20

GLOSSARY OF LEGAL TERMS

A

ACTION - "Action" includes a civil action and a criminal action.
A FORTIORI - A term meaning you can reason one thing from the existence of certain facts.
A POSTERIORI - From what goes after; from effect to cause.
A PRIORI - From what goes before; from cause to effect.
AB INITIO - From the beginning.
ABATE - To diminish or put an end to.
ABET - To encourage the commission of a crime.
ABEYANCE - Suspension, temporary suppression.
ABIDE - To accept the consequences of.
ABJURE - To renounce; give up.
ABRIDGE - To reduce; contract; diminish.
ABROGATE - To annul, repeal, or destroy.
ABSCOND - To hide or absent oneself to avoid legal action.
ABSTRACT - A summary.
ABUT - To border on, to touch.
ACCESS - Approach; in real property law it means the right of the owner of property to the use of the highway or road next to his land, without obstruction by intervening property owners.
ACCESSORY - In criminal law, it means the person who contributes or aids in the commission of a crime.
ACCOMMODATED PARTY - One to whom credit is extended on the strength of another person signing a commercial paper.
ACCOMMODATION PAPER - A commercial paper to which the accommodating party has put his name.
ACCOMPLICE - In criminal law, it means a person who together with the principal offender commits a crime.
ACCORD - An agreement to accept something different or less than that to which one is entitled, which extinguishes the entire obligation.
ACCOUNT - A statement of mutual demands in the nature of debt and credit between parties.
ACCRETION - The act of adding to a thing; in real property law, it means gradual accumulation of land by natural causes.
ACCRUE - To grow to; to be added to.
ACKNOWLEDGMENT - The act of going before an official authorized to take acknowledgments, and acknowledging an act as one's own.
ACQUIESCENCE - A silent appearance of consent.
ACQUIT - To legally determine the innocence of one charged with a crime.
AD INFINITUM - Indefinitely.
AD LITEM - For the suit.
AD VALOREM - According to value.
ADJECTIVE LAW - Rules of procedure.
ADJUDICATION - The judgment given in a case.
ADMIRALTY - Court having jurisdiction over maritime cases.
ADULT - Sixteen years old or over (in criminal law).
ADVANCE - In commercial law, it means to pay money or render other value before it is due.
ADVERSE - Opposed; contrary.
ADVOCATE - (v.) To speak in favor of;
 (n.) One who assists, defends, or pleads for another.
AFFIANT - A person who makes and signs an affidavit.

AFFIDAVIT - A written and sworn to declaration of facts, voluntarily made.
AFFINITY- The relationship between persons through marriage with the kindred of each other; distinguished from consanguinity, which is the relationship by blood.
AFFIRM - To ratify; also when an appellate court affirms a judgment, decree, or order, it means that it is valid and right and must stand as rendered in the lower court.
AFOREMENTIONED; AFORESAID - Before or already said.
AGENT - One who represents and acts for another.
AID AND COMFORT - To help; encourage.
ALIAS - A name not one's true name.
ALIBI - A claim of not being present at a certain place at a certain time.
ALLEGE - To assert.
ALLOTMENT - A share or portion.
AMBIGUITY - Uncertainty; capable of being understood in more than one way.
AMENDMENT - Any language made or proposed as a change in some principal writing.
AMICUS CURIAE - A friend of the court; one who has an interest in a case, although not a party in the case, who volunteers advice upon matters of law to the judge. For example, a brief amicus curiae.
AMORTIZATION - To provide for a gradual extinction of (a future obligation) in advance of maturity, especially, by periodical contributions to a sinking fund which will be adequate to discharge a debt or make a replacement when it becomes necessary.
ANCILLARY - Aiding, auxiliary.
ANNOTATION - A note added by way of comment or explanation.
ANSWER - A written statement made by a defendant setting forth the grounds of his defense.
ANTE - Before.
ANTE MORTEM - Before death.
APPEAL - The removal of a case from a lower court to one of superior jurisdiction for the purpose of obtaining a review.
APPEARANCE - Coming into court as a party to a suit.
APPELLANT - The party who takes an appeal from one court or jurisdiction to another (appellate) court for review.
APPELLEE - The party against whom an appeal is taken.
APPROPRIATE - To make a thing one's own.
APPROPRIATION - Prescribing the destination of a thing; the act of the legislature designating a particular fund, to be applied to some object of government expenditure.
APPURTENANT - Belonging to; accessory or incident to.
ARBITER - One who decides a dispute; a referee.
ARBITRARY - Unreasoned; not governed by any fixed rules or standard.
ARGUENDO - By way of argument.
ARRAIGN - To call the prisoner before the court to answer to a charge.
ASSENT - A declaration of willingness to do something in compliance with a request.
ASSERT - Declare.
ASSESS - To fix the rate or amount.
ASSIGN - To transfer; to appoint; to select for a particular purpose.
ASSIGNEE - One who receives an assignment.
ASSIGNOR - One who makes an assignment.
AT BAR - Before the court.

AT ISSUE - When parties in an action come to a point where one asserts something and the other denies it.
ATTACH - Seize property by court order and sometimes arrest a person.
ATTEST - To witness a will, etc.; act of attestation.
AVERMENT - A positive statement of facts.

B

BAIL - To obtain the release of a person from legal custody by giving security and promising that he shall appear in court; to deliver (goods, etc.) in trust to a person for a special purpose.
BAILEE - One to whom personal property is delivered under a contract of bailment.
BAILMENT - Delivery of personal property to another to be held for a certain purpose and to be returned when the purpose is accomplished.
BAILOR - The party who delivers goods to another, under a contract of bailment.
BANC (OR BANK) - Bench; the place where a court sits permanently or regularly; also the assembly of all the judges of a court.
BANKRUPT - An insolvent person, technically, one declared to be bankrupt after a bankruptcy proceeding.
BAR - The legal profession.
BARRATRY - Exciting groundless judicial proceedings.
BARTER - A contract by which parties exchange goods for other goods.
BATTERY - Illegal interfering with another's person.
BEARER - In commercial law, it means the person in possession of a commercial paper which is payable to the bearer.
BENCH - The court itself or the judge.
BENEFICIARY - A person benefiting under a will, trust, or agreement.
BEST EVIDENCE RULE, THE - Except as otherwise provided by statute, no evidence other than the writing itself is admissible to prove the content of a writing. This section shall be known and may be cited as the best evidence rule.
BEQUEST - A gift of personal property under a will.
BILL - A formal written statement of complaint to a court of justice; also, a draft of an act of the legislature before it becomes a law; also, accounts for goods sold, services rendered, or work done.
BONA FIDE - In or with good faith; honestly.
BOND - An instrument by which the maker promises to pay a sum of money to another, usually providing that upon performances of a certain condition the obligation shall be void.
BOYCOTT - A plan to prevent the carrying on of a business by wrongful means.
BREACH - The breaking or violating of a law, or the failure to carry out a duty.
BRIEF - A written document, prepared by a lawyer to serve as the basis of an argument upon a case in court, usually an appellate court.
BURDEN OF PRODUCING EVIDENCE - The obligation of a party to introduce evidence sufficient to avoid a ruling against him on the issue.
BURDEN OF PROOF - The obligation of a party to establish by evidence a requisite degree of belief concerning a fact in the mind of the trier of fact or the court. The burden of proof may require a party to raise a reasonable doubt concerning the existence of nonexistence of a fact or that he establish the existence or nonexistence of a fact by a preponderance of the evidence, by clear and convincing proof, or by proof beyond a reasonable doubt.

Except as otherwise provided by law, the burden of proof requires proof by a preponderance of the evidence.

BUSINESS, A - Shall include every kind of business, profession, occupation, calling or operation of institutions, whether carried on for profit or not.

BY-LAWS - Regulations, ordinances, or rules enacted by a corporation, association, etc., for its own government.

C

CANON - A doctrine; also, a law or rule, of a church or association in particular.

CAPIAS - An order to arrest.

CAPTION - In a pleading, deposition or other paper connected with a case in court, it is the heading or introductory clause which shows the names of the parties, name of the court, number of the case on the docket or calendar, etc.

CARRIER - A person or corporation undertaking to transport persons or property.

CASE - A general term for an action, cause, suit, or controversy before a judicial body.

CAUSE - A suit, litigation or action before a court.

CAVEAT EMPTOR - Let the buyer beware. This term expresses the rule that the purchaser of an article must examine, judge, and test it for himself, being bound to discover any obvious defects or imperfections.

CERTIFICATE - A written representation that some legal formality has been complied with.

CERTIORARI - To be informed of; the name of a writ issued by a superior court directing the lower court to send up to the former the record and proceedings of a case.

CHANGE OF VENUE - To remove place of trial from one place to another.

CHARGE - An obligation or duty; a formal complaint; an instruction of the court to the jury upon a case.

CHARTER - (n.) The authority by virtue of which an organized body acts;
(v.) in mercantile law, it means to hire or lease a vehicle or vessel for transportation.

CHATTEL - An article of personal property.

CHATTEL MORTGAGE - A mortgage on personal property.

CIRCUIT - A division of the country, for the administration of justice; a geographical area served by a court.

CITATION - The act of the court by which a person is summoned or cited; also, a reference to legal authority.

CIVIL (ACTIONS)- It indicates the private rights and remedies of individuals in contrast to the word "criminal" (actions) which relates to prosecution for violation of laws.

CLAIM (n.) - Any demand held or asserted as of right.

CODICIL - An addition to a will.

CODIFY - To arrange the laws of a country into a code.

COGNIZANCE - Notice or knowledge.

COLLATERAL - By the side; accompanying; an article or thing given to secure performance of a promise.

COMITY - Courtesy; the practice by which one court follows the decision of another court on the same question.

COMMIT - To perform, as an act; to perpetrate, as a crime; to send a person to prison.

COMMON LAW - As distinguished from law created by the enactment of the legislature (called statutory law), it relates to those principles and rules of action which derive their authority solely from usages and customs of immemorial antiquity, particularly with reference to the ancient unwritten law of England. The written pronouncements of the common law are found in court decisions.

COMMUTE - Change punishment to one less severe.

COMPLAINANT - One who applies to the court for legal redress.
COMPLAINT - The pleading of a plaintiff in a civil action; or a charge that a person has committed a specified offense.
COMPROMISE - An arrangement for settling a dispute by agreement.
CONCUR - To agree, consent.
CONCURRENT - Running together, at the same time.
CONDEMNATION - Taking private property for public use on payment therefor.
CONDITION - Mode or state of being; a qualification or restriction.
CONDUCT - Active and passive behavior; both verbal and nonverbal.
CONFESSION - Voluntary statement of guilt of crime.
CONFIDENTIAL COMMUNICATION BETWEEN CLIENT AND LAWYER - Information transmitted between a client and his lawyer in the course of that relationship and in confidence by a means which, so far as the client is aware, discloses the information to no third persons other than those who are present to further the interest of the client in the consultation or those to whom disclosure is reasonably necessary for the transmission of the information or the accomplishment of the purpose for which the lawyer is consulted, and includes a legal opinion formed and the advice given by the lawyer in the course of that relationship.
CONFRONTATION - Witness testifying in presence of defendant.
CONSANGUINITY - Blood relationship.
CONSIGN - To give in charge; commit; entrust; to send or transmit goods to a merchant, factor, or agent for sale.
CONSIGNEE - One to whom a consignment is made.
CONSIGNOR - One who sends or makes a consignment.
CONSPIRACY - In criminal law, it means an agreement between two or more persons to commit an unlawful act.
CONSPIRATORS - Persons involved in a conspiracy.
CONSTITUTION - The fundamental law of a nation or state.
CONSTRUCTION OF GENDERS - The masculine gender includes the feminine and neuter.
CONSTRUCTION OF SINGULAR AND PLURAL - The singular number includes the plural; and the plural, the singular.
CONSTRUCTION OF TENSES - The present tense includes the past and future tenses; and the future, the present.
CONSTRUCTIVE - An act or condition assumed from other parts or conditions.
CONSTRUE - To ascertain the meaning of language.
CONSUMMATE - To complete.
CONTIGUOUS - Adjoining; touching; bounded by.
CONTINGENT - Possible, but not assured; dependent upon some condition.
CONTINUANCE - The adjournment or postponement of an action pending in a court.
CONTRA - Against, opposed to; contrary.
CONTRACT - An agreement between two or more persons to do or not to do a particular thing.
CONTROVERT - To dispute, deny.
CONVERSION - Dealing with the personal property of another as if it were one's own, without right.
CONVEYANCE - An instrument transferring title to land.
CONVICTION - Generally, the result of a criminal trial which ends in a judgment or sentence that the defendant is guilty as charged.

COOPERATIVE - A cooperative is a voluntary organization of persons with a common interest, formed and operated along democratic lines for the purpose of supplying services at cost to its members and other patrons, who contribute both capital and business.
CORPUS DELICTI - The body of a crime; the crime itself.
CORROBORATE - To strengthen; to add weight by additional evidence.
COUNTERCLAIM - A claim presented by a defendant in opposition to or deduction from the claim of the plaintiff.
COUNTY - Political subdivision of a state.
COVENANT - Agreement.
CREDIBLE - Worthy of belief.
CREDITOR - A person to whom a debt is owing by another person, called the "debtor."
CRIMINAL ACTION - Includes criminal proceedings.
CRIMINAL INFORMATION - Same as complaint.
CRITERION (sing.)
CRITERIA (plural) - A means or tests for judging; a standard or standards.
CROSS-EXAMINATION - Examination of a witness by a party other than the direct examiner upon a matter that is within the scope of the direct examination of the witness.
CULPABLE - Blamable.
CY-PRES - As near as (possible). The rule of *cy-pres* is a rule for the construction of instruments in equity by which the intention of the party is carried out *as near as may be*, when it would be impossible or illegal to give it literal effect.

D

DAMAGES - A monetary compensation, which may be recovered in the courts by any person who has suffered loss, or injury, whether to his person, property or rights through the unlawful act or omission or negligence of another.
DECLARANT - A person who makes a statement.
DE FACTO - In fact; actually but without legal authority.
DE JURE - Of right; legitimate; lawful.
DE MINIMIS - Very small or trifling.
DE NOVO - Anew; afresh; a second time.
DEBT - A specified sum of money owing to one person from another, including not only the obligation of the debtor to pay, but the right of the creditor to receive and enforce payment.
DECEDENT - A dead person.
DECISION - A judgment or decree pronounced by a court in determination of a case.
DECREE - An order of the court, determining the rights of all parties to a suit.
DEED - A writing containing a contract sealed and delivered; particularly to convey real property.
DEFALCATION - Misappropriation of funds.
DEFAMATION - Injuring one's reputation by false statements.
DEFAULT - The failure to fulfill a duty, observe a promise, discharge an obligation, or perform an agreement.
DEFENDANT - The person defending or denying; the party against whom relief or recovery is sought in an action or suit.
DEFRAUD - To practice fraud; to cheat or trick.
DELEGATE (v.)- To entrust to the care or management of another.
DELICTUS - A crime.
DEMUR (v.) - To dispute the sufficiency in law of the pleading of the other side.

DEMURRAGE - In maritime law, it means, the sum fixed or allowed as remuneration to the owners of a ship for the detention of their vessel beyond the number of days allowed for loading and unloading or for sailing; also used in railroad terminology.
DENIAL - A form of pleading; refusing to admit the truth of a statement, charge, etc.
DEPONENT - One who gives testimony under oath reduced to writing.
DEPOSITION - Testimony given under oath outside of court for use in court or for the purpose of obtaining information in preparation for trial of a case.
DETERIORATION - A degeneration such as from decay, corrosion or disintegration.
DETRIMENT - Any loss or harm to person or property.
DEVIATION - A turning aside.
DEVISE - A gift of real property by the last will and testament of the donor.
DICTUM (sing.)
DICTA (plural) - Any statements made by the court in an opinion concerning some rule of law not necessarily involved nor essential to the determination of the case.
DIRECT EVIDENCE - Evidence that directly proves a fact, without an inference or presumption, and which in itself if true, conclusively establishes that fact.
DIRECT EXAMINATION - The first examination of a witness upon a matter that is not within the scope of a previous examination of the witness.
DISAFFIRM - To repudiate.
DISMISS - In an action or suit, it means to dispose of the case without any further consideration or hearing.
DISSENT - To denote disagreement of one or more judges of a court with the decision passed by the majority upon a case before them.
DOCKET (n.) - A formal record, entered in brief, of the proceedings in a court.
DOCTRINE - A rule, principle, theory of law.
DOMICILE - That place where a man has his true, fixed and permanent home to which whenever he is absent he has the intention of returning.
DRAFT (n.) - A commercial paper ordering payment of money drawn by one person on another.
DRAWEE - The person who is requested to pay the money.
DRAWER - The person who draws the commercial paper and addresses it to the drawee.
DUPLICATE - A counterpart produced by the same impression as the original enlargements and miniatures, or by mechanical or electronic re-recording, or by chemical reproduction, or by other equivalent technique which accurately reproduces the original.
DURESS - Use of force to compel performance or non-performance of an act.

E

EASEMENT - A liberty, privilege, or advantage without profit, in the lands of another.
EGRESS - Act or right of going out or leaving; emergence.
EIUSDEM GENERIS - Of the same kind, class or nature. A rule used in the construction of language in a legal document.
EMBEZZLEMENT - To steal; to appropriate fraudulently to one's own use property entrusted to one's care.
EMBRACERY - Unlawful attempt to influence jurors, etc., but not by offering value.
EMINENT DOMAIN - The right of a state to take private property for public use.
ENACT - To make into a law.
ENDORSEMENT - Act of writing one's name on the back of a note, bill or similar written instrument.

ENJOIN - To require a person, by writ of injunction from a court of equity, to perform or to abstain or desist from some act.
ENTIRETY - The whole; that which the law considers as one whole, and not capable of being divided into parts.
ENTRAPMENT - Inducing one to commit a crime so as to arrest him.
ENUMERATED - Mentioned specifically; designated.
ENURE - To operate or take effect.
EQUITY - In its broadest sense, this term denotes the spirit and the habit of fairness, justness, and right dealing which regulate the conduct of men.
ERROR - A mistake of law, or the false or irregular application of law as will nullify the judicial proceedings.
ESCROW - A deed, bond or other written engagement, delivered to a third person, to be delivered by him only upon the performance or fulfillment of some condition.
ESTATE - The interest which any one has in lands, or in any other subject of property.
ESTOP - To stop, bar, or impede.
ESTOPPEL - A rule of law which prevents a man from alleging or denying a fact, because of his own previous act.
ET AL. (alii) - And others.
ET SEQ. (sequential) - And the following.
ET UX. (uxor) - And wife.
EVIDENCE - Testimony, writings, material objects, or other things presented to the senses that are offered to prove the existence or non-existence of a fact.
  Means from which inferences may be drawn as a basis of proof in duly constituted judicial or fact finding tribunals, and includes testimony in the form of opinion and hearsay.
EX CONTRACTU
EX DELICTO - In law, rights and causes of action are divided into two classes, those arising *ex contractu* (from a contract) and those arising *ex delicto* (from a delict or tort).
EX OFFICIO - From office; by virtue of the office.
EX PARTE - On one side only; by or for one.
EX POST FACTO - After the fact.
EX POST FACTO LAW - A law passed after an act was done which retroactively makes such act a crime.
EX REL. (relations) - Upon relation or information.
EXCEPTION - An objection upon a matter of law to a decision made, either before or after judgment by a court.
EXECUTOR (male)
EXECUTRIX (female) - A person who has been appointed by will to execute the will.
EXECUTORY - That which is yet to be executed or performed.
EXEMPT - To release from some liability to which others are subject.
EXONERATION - The removal of a burden, charge or duty.
EXTRADITION - Surrender of a fugitive from one nation to another.

F

F.A.S.- "Free alongside ship"; delivery at dock for ship named.
F.O.B.- "Free on board"; seller will deliver to car, truck, vessel, or other conveyance by which goods are to be transported, without expense or risk of loss to the buyer or consignee.
FABRICATE - To construct; to invent a false story.
FACSIMILE - An exact or accurate copy of an original instrument.

FACTOR - A commercial agent.
FEASANCE - The doing of an act.
FELONIOUS - Criminal, malicious.
FELONY - Generally, a criminal offense that may be punished by death or imprisonment for more than one year as differentiated from a misdemeanor.
FEME SOLE - A single woman.
FIDUCIARY - A person who is invested with rights and powers to be exercised for the benefit of another person.
FIERI FACIAS - A writ of execution commanding the sheriff to levy and collect the amount of a judgment from the goods and chattels of the judgment debtor.
FINDING OF FACT - Determination from proof or judicial notice of the existence of a fact. A ruling implies a supporting finding of fact; no separate or formal finding is required unless required by a statute of this state.
FISCAL - Relating to accounts or the management of revenue.
FORECLOSURE (sale) - A sale of mortgaged property to obtain satisfaction of the mortgage out of the sale proceeds.
FORFEITURE - A penalty, a fine.
FORGERY - Fabricating or producing falsely, counterfeited.
FORTUITOUS - Accidental.
FORUM - A court of justice; a place of jurisdiction.
FRAUD - Deception; trickery.
FREEHOLDER - One who owns real property.
FUNGIBLE - Of such kind or nature that one specimen or part may be used in the place of another.

G

GARNISHEE - Person garnished.
GARNISHMENT - A legal process to reach the money or effects of a defendant, in the possession or control of a third person.
GRAND JURY - Not less than 16, not more than 23 citizens of a county sworn to inquire into crimes committed or triable in the county.
GRANT - To agree to; convey, especially real property.
GRANTEE - The person to whom a grant is made.
GRANTOR - The person by whom a grant is made.
GRATUITOUS - Given without a return, compensation or consideration.
GRAVAMEN - The grievance complained of or the substantial cause of a criminal action.
GUARANTY (n.) - A promise to answer for the payment of some debt, or the performance of some duty, in case of the failure of another person, who, in the first instance, is liable for such payment or performance.
GUARDIAN - The person, committee, or other representative authorized by law to protect the person or estate or both of an incompetent (or of a *sui juris* person having a guardian) and to act for him in matters affecting his person or property or both. An incompetent is a person under disability imposed by law.
GUILTY - Establishment of the fact that one has committed a breach of conduct; especially, a violation of law.

H

HABEAS CORPUS - You have the body; the name given to a variety of writs, having for their object to bring a party before a court or judge for decision as to whether such person is being lawfully held prisoner.
HABENDUM - In conveyancing; it is the clause in a deed conveying land which defines the extent of ownership to be held by the grantee.
HEARING - A proceeding whereby the arguments of the interested parties are heared.
HEARSAY - A type of testimony given by a witness who relates, not what he knows personally, but what others have told hi, or what he has heard said by others.
HEARSAY RULE, THE - (a) "Hearsay evidence" is evidence of a statement that was made other than by a witness while testifying at the hearing and that is offered to prove the truth of the matter stated; (b) Except as provided by law, hearsay evidence is inadmissible; (c) This section shall be known and may be cited as the hearsay rule.
HEIR - Generally, one who inherits property, real or personal.
HOLDER OF THE PRIVILEGE - (a) The client when he has no guardian or conservator; (b) A guardian or conservator of the client when the client has a guardian or conservator; (c) The personal representative of the client if the client is dead; (d) A successor, assign, trustee in dissolution, or any similar representative of a firm, association, organization, partnership, business trust, corporation, or public entity that is no longer in existence.
HUNG JURY - One so divided that they can't agree on a verdict.
HUSBAND-WIFE PRIVILEGE - An accused in a criminal proceeding has a privilege to prevent his spouse from testifying against him.
HYPOTHECATE - To pledge a thing without delivering it to the pledgee.
HYPOTHESIS - A supposition, assumption, or toehry.

I

I.E. (id est) - That is.
IB., OR IBID.(ibidem) - In the same place; used to refer to a legal reference previously cited to avoid repeating the entire citation.
ILLICIT - Prohibited; unlawful.
ILLUSORY - Deceiving by false appearance.
IMMUNITY - Exemption.
IMPEACH - To accuse, to dispute.
IMPEDIMENTS - Disabilities, or hindrances.
IMPLEAD - To sue or prosecute by due course of law.
IMPUTED - Attributed or charged to.
IN LOCO PARENTIS - In place of parent, a guardian.
IN TOTO - In the whole; completely.
INCHOATE - Imperfect; unfinished.
INCOMMUNICADO - Denial of the right of a prisoner to communicate with friends or relatives.
INCOMPETENT - One who is incapable of caring for his own affairs because he is mentally deficient or undeveloped.
INCRIMINATION - A matter will incriminate a person if it constitutes, or forms an essential part of, or, taken in connection with other matters disclosed, is a basis for a reasonable inference of such a violation of the laws of this State as to subject him to liability to punishment therefor, unless he has become for any reason permanently immune from punishment for such violation.
INCUMBRANCE - Generally a claim, lien, charge or liability attached to and binding real property.

INDEMNIFY - To secure against loss or damage; also, to make reimbursement to one for a loss already incurred by him.
INDEMNITY - An agreement to reimburse another person in case of an anticipated loss falling upon him.
INDICIA - Signs; indications.
INDICTMENT - An accusation in writing found and presented by a grand jury charging that a person has committed a crime.
INDORSE - To write a name on the back of a legal paper or document, generally, a negotiable instrument
INDUCEMENT - Cause or reason why a thing is done or that which incites the person to do the act or commit a crime; the motive for the criminal act.
INFANT - In civil cases one under 21 years of age.
INFORMATION - A formal accusation of crime made by a prosecuting attorney.
INFRA - Below, under; this word occurring by itself in a publication refers the reader to a future part of the publication.
INGRESS - The act of going into.
INJUNCTION - A writ or order by the court requiring a person, generally, to do or to refrain from doing an act.
INSOLVENT - The condition of a person who is unable to pay his debts.
INSTRUCTION - A direction given by the judge to the jury concerning the law of the case.
INTERIM - In the meantime; time intervening.
INTERLOCUTORY - Temporary, not final; something intervening between the commencement and the end of a suit which decides some point or matter, but is not a final decision of the whole controversy.
INTERROGATORIES - A series of formal written questions used in the examination of a party or a witness usually prior to a trial.
INTESTATE - A person who dies without a will.
INURE - To result, to take effect.
IPSO FACTO - By the fact iself; by the mere fact.
ISSUE (n.) The disputed point or question in a case,

J

JEOPARDY - Danger, hazard, peril.
JOINDER - Joining; uniting with another person in some legal steps or proceeding.
JOINT - United; combined.
JUDGE - Member or members or representative or representatives of a court conducting a trial or hearing at which evidence is introduced.
JUDGMENT - The official decision of a court of justice.
JUDICIAL OR JUDICIARY - Relating to or connected with the administration of justice.
JURAT - The clause written at the foot of an affidavit, stating when, where and before whom such affidavit was sworn.
JURISDICTION - The authority to hear and determine controversies between parties.
JURISPRUDENCE - The philosophy of law.
JURY - A body of persons legally selected to inquire into any matter of fact, and to render their verdict according to the evidence.

L

LACHES - The failure to diligently assert a right, which results in a refusal to allow relief.

LANDLORD AND TENANT - A phrase used to denote the legal relation existing between the owner and occupant of real estate.
LARCENY - Stealing personal property belonging to another.
LATENT - Hidden; that which does not appear on the face of a thing.
LAW - Includes constitutional, statutory, and decisional law.
LAWYER-CLIENT PRIVILEGE - (1) A "client" is a person, public officer, or corporation, association, or other organization or entity, either public or private, who is rendered professional legal services by a lawyer, or who consults a lawyer with a view to obtaining professional legal services from him; (2) A "lawyer" is a person authorized, or reasonably believed by the client to be authorized, to practice law in any state or nation; (3) A "representative of the lawyer" is one employed to assist the lawyer in the rendition of professional legal services; (4) A communication is "confidential" if not intended to be disclosed to third persons other than those to whom disclosure is in furtherance of the rendition of professional legal services to the client or those reasonably necessary for the transmission of the communication.

General rule of privilege - A client has a privilege to refuse to disclose and to prevent any other person from disclosing confidential communications made for the purpose of facilitating the rendition of professional legal services to the client, (1) between himself or his representative and his lawyer or his lawyer's representative, or (2) between his lawyer and the lawyer's representative, or (3) by him or his lawyer to a lawyer representing another in a matter of common interest, or (4) between representatives of the client or between the client and a representative of the client, or (5) between lawyers representing the client.
LEADING QUESTION - Question that suggests to the witness the answer that the examining party desires.
LEASE - A contract by which one conveys real estate for a limited time usually for a specified rent; personal property also may be leased.
LEGISLATION - The act of enacting laws.
LEGITIMATE - Lawful.
LESSEE - One to whom a lease is given.
LESSOR - One who grants a lease
LEVY - A collecting or exacting by authority.
LIABLE - Responsible; bound or obligated in law or equity.
LIBEL (v.) - To defame or injure a person's reputation by a published writing.
    (n.) - The initial pleading on the part of the plaintiff in an admiralty proceeding.
LIEN - A hold or claim which one person has upon the property of another as a security for some debt or charge.
LIQUIDATED - Fixed; settled.
LIS PENDENS - A pending civil or criminal action.
LITERAL - According to the language.
LITIGANT - A party to a lawsuit.
LITATION - A judicial controversy.
LOCUS - A place.
LOCUS DELICTI - Place of the crime.
LOCUS POENITENTIAE - The abandoning or giving up of one's intention to commit some crime before it is fully completed or abandoning a conspiracy before its purpose is accomplished.

M

MALFEASANCE - To do a wrongful act.
MALICE - The doing of a wrongful act Intentionally without just cause or excuse.

MANDAMUS - The name of a writ issued by a court to enforce the performance of some public duty.
MANDATORY (adj.) Containing a command.
MARITIME - Pertaining to the sea or to commerce thereon.
MARSHALING - Arranging or disposing of in order.
MAXIM - An established principle or proposition.
MINISTERIAL - That which involves obedience to instruction, but demands no special discretion, judgment or skill.
MISAPPROPRIATE - Dealing fraudulently with property entrusted to one.
MISDEMEANOR - A crime less than a felony and punishable by a fine or imprisonment for less than one year.
MISFEASANCE - Improper performance of a lawful act.
MISREPRESENTATION - An untrue representation of facts.
MITIGATE - To make or become less severe, harsh.
MITTIMUS - A warrant of commitment to prison.
MOOT (adj.) Unsettled, undecided, not necessary to be decided.
MORTGAGE - A conveyance of property upon condition, as security for the payment of a debt or the performance of a duty, and to become void upon payment or performance according to the stipulated terms.
MORTGAGEE - A person to whom property is mortgaged.
MORTGAGOR - One who gives a mortgage.
MOTION - In legal proceedings, a "motion" is an application, either written or oral, addressed to the court by a party to an action or a suit requesting the ruling of the court on a matter of law.
MUTUALITY - Reciprocation.

N

NEGLIGENCE - The failure to exercise that degree of care which an ordinarily prudent person would exercise under like circumstances.
NEGOTIABLE (instrument) - Any instrument obligating the payment of money which is transferable from one person to another by endorsement and delivery or by delivery only.
NEGOTIATE - To transact business; to transfer a negotiable instrument; to seek agreement for the amicable disposition of a controversy or case.
NOLLE PROSEQUI - A formal entry upon the record, by the plaintiff in a civil suit or the prosecuting officer in a criminal action, by which he declares that he "will no further prosecute" the case.
NOLO CONTENDERE - The name of a plea in a criminal action, having the same effect as a plea of guilty; but not constituting a direct admission of guilt.
NOMINAL - Not real or substantial.
NOMINAL DAMAGES - Award of a trifling sum where no substantial injury is proved to have been sustained.
NONFEASANCE - Neglect of duty.
NOVATION - The substitution of a new debt or obligation for an existing one.
NUNC PRO TUNC - A phrase applied to acts allowed to be done after the time when they should be done, with a retroactive effect.("Now for then.")

O

OATH - Oath includes affirmation or declaration under penalty of perjury.
OBITER DICTUM - Opinion expressed by a court on a matter not essentially involved in a case and hence not a decision; also called dicta, if plural.

OBJECT (v.) - To oppose as improper or illegal and referring the question of its propriety or legality to the court.
OBLIGATION - A legal duty, by which a person is bound to do or not to do a certain thing.
OBLIGEE - The person to whom an obligation is owed.
OBLIGOR - The person who is to perform the obligation.
OFFER (v.) - To present for acceptance or rejection.
　　　(n.) - A proposal to do a thing, usually a proposal to make a contract.
OFFICIAL INFORMATION - Information within the custody or control of a department or agency of the government the disclosure of which is shown to be contrary to the public interest.
OFFSET - A deduction.
ONUS PROBANDI - Burden of proof.
OPINION - The statement by a judge of the decision reached in a case, giving the law as applied to the case and giving reasons for the judgment; also a belief or view.
OPTION - The exercise of the power of choice; also a privilege existing in one person, for which he has paid money, which gives him the right to buy or sell real or personal property at a given price within a specified time.
ORDER - A rule or regulation; every direction of a court or judge made or entered in writing but not including a judgment.
ORDINANCE - Generally, a rule established by authority; also commonly used to designate the legislative acts of a municipal corporation.
ORIGINAL - Writing or recording itself or any counterpart intended to have the same effect by a person executing or issuing it. An "original" of a photograph includes the negative or any print therefrom. If data are stored in a computer or similar device, any printout or other output readable by sight, shown to reflect the data accurately, is an "original."
OVERT - Open, manifest.

P

PANEL - A group of jurors selected to serve during a term of the court.
PARENS PATRIAE - Sovereign power of a state to protect or be a guardian over children and incompetents.
PAROL - Oral or verbal.
PAROLE - To release one in prison before the expiration of his sentence, conditionally.
PARITY - Equality in purchasing power between the farmer and other segments of the economy.
PARTITION - A legal division of real or personal property between one or more owners.
PARTNERSHIP - An association of two or more persons to carry on as co-owners a business for profit.
PATENT (adj.) - Evident.
　　　(n.) - A grant of some privilege, property, or authority, made by the government or sovereign of a country to one or more individuals.
PECULATION - Stealing.
PECUNIARY - Monetary.
PENULTIMATE - Next to the last.
PER CURIAM - A phrase used in the report of a decision to distinguish an opinion of the whole court from an opinion written by any one judge.
PER SE - In itself; taken alone.
PERCEIVE - To acquire knowledge through one's senses.
PEREMPTORY - Imperative; absolute.
PERJURY - To lie or state falsely under oath.

PERPETUITY - Perpetual existence; also the quality or condition of an estate limited so that it will not take effect or vest within the period fixed by law.
PERSON - Includes a natural person, firm, association, organization, partnership, business trust, corporation, or public entity.
PERSONAL PROPERTY - Includes money, goods, chattels, things in action, and evidences of debt.
PERSONALTY - Short term for personal property.
PETITION - An application in writing for an order of the court, stating the circumstances upon which it is founded and requesting any order or other relief from a court.
PLAINTIFF - A person who brings a court action.
PLEA - A pleading in a suit or action.
PLEADINGS - Formal allegations made by the parties of their respective claims and defenses, for the judgment of the court.
PLEDGE - A deposit of personal property as a security for the performance of an act.
PLEDGEE - The party to whom goods are delivered in pledge.
PLEDGOR - The party delivering goods in pledge.
PLENARY - Full; complete.
POLICE POWER - Inherent power of the state or its political subdivisions to enact laws within constitutional limits to promote the general welfare of society or the community.
POLLING THE JURY - Call the names of persons on a jury and requiring each juror to declare what his verdict is before it is legally recorded.
POST MORTEM - After death.
POWER OF ATTORNEY - A writing authorizing one to act for another.
PRECEPT - An order, warrant, or writ issued to an officer or body of officers, commanding him or them to do some act within the scope of his or their powers.
PRELIMINARY FACT - Fact upon the existence or nonexistence of which depends the admissibility or inadmissibility of evidence. The phrase "the admissibility or inadmissibility of evidence" includes the qualification or disqualification of a person to be a witness and the existence or nonexistence of a privilege.
PREPONDERANCE - Outweighing.
PRESENTMENT - A report by a grand jury on something they have investigated on their own knowledge.
PRESUMPTION - An assumption of fact resulting from a rule of law which requires such fact to be assumed from another fact or group of facts found or otherwise established in the action.
PRIMA FACUE - At first sight.
PRIMA FACIE CASE - A case where the evidence is very patent against the defendant.
PRINCIPAL - The source of authority or rights; a person primarily liable as differentiated from "principle" as a primary or basic doctrine.
PRO AND CON - For and against.
PRO RATA - Proportionally.
PROBATE - Relating to proof, especially to the proof of wills.
PROBATIVE - Tending to prove.
PROCEDURE - In law, this term generally denotes rules which are established by the Federal, State, or local Governments regarding the types of pleading and courtroom practice which must be followed by the parties involved in a criminal or civil case.
PROCLAMATION - A public notice by an official of some order, intended action, or state of facts.

PROFFERED EVIDENCE - The admissibility or inadmissibility of which is dependent upon the existence or nonexistence of a preliminary fact.
PROMISSORY (NOTE) - A promise in writing to pay a specified sum at an expressed time, or on demand, or at sight, to a named person, or to his order, or bearer.
PROOF - The establishment by evidence of a requisite degree of belief concerning a fact in the mind of the trier of fact or the court.
PROPERTY - Includes both real and personal property.
PROPRIETARY (adj.) - Relating or pertaining to ownership; usually a single owner.
PROSECUTE - To carry on an action or other judicial proceeding; to proceed against a person criminally.
PROVISO - A limitation or condition in a legal instrument.
PROXIMATE - Immediate; nearest
PUBLIC EMPLOYEE - An officer, agent, or employee of a public entity.
PUBLIC ENTITY - Includes a national, state, county, city and county, city, district, public authority, public agency, or any other political subdivision or public corporation, whether foreign or domestic.
PUBLIC OFFICIAL - Includes an official of a political dubdivision of such state or territory and of a municipality.
PUNITIVE - Relating to punishment.

Q

QUASH - To make void.
QUASI - As if; as it were.
QUID PRO QUO - Something for something; the giving of one valuable thing for another.
QUITCLAIM (v.) - To release or relinquish claim or title to, especially in deeds to realty.
QUO WARRANTO - A legal procedure to test an official's right to a public office or the right to hold a franchise, or to hold an office in a domestic corporation.

R

RATIFY - To approve and sanction.
REAL PROPERTY - Includes lands, tenements, and hereditaments.
REALTY - A brief term for real property.
REBUT - To contradict; to refute, especially by evidence and arguments.
RECEIVER - A person who is appointed by the court to receive, and hold in trust property in litigation.
RECIDIVIST - Habitual criminal.
RECIPROCAL - Mutual.
RECOUPMENT - To keep back or get something which is due; also, it is the right of a defendant to have a deduction from the amount of the plaintiff's damages because the plaintiff has not fulfilled his part of the same contract.
RECROSS EXAMINATION - Examination of a witness by a cross-examiner subsequent to a redirect examination of the witness.
REDEEM - To release an estate or article from mortgage or pledge by paying the debt for which it stood as security.
REDIRECT EXAMINATION - Examination of a witness by the direct examiner subsequent to the cross-examination of the witness.
REFEREE - A person to whom a cause pending in a court is referred by the court, to take testimony, hear the parties, and report thereon to the court.

REFERENDUM - A method of submitting an important legislative or administrative matter to a direct vote of the people.
RELEVANT EVIDENCE - Evidence including evidence relevant to the credulity of a witness or hearsay declarant, having any tendency in reason to prove or disprove any disputed fact that is of consequence to the determination of the action.
REMAND - To send a case back to the lower court from which it came, for further proceedings.
REPLEVIN - An action to recover goods or chattels wrongfully taken or detained.
REPLY (REPLICATION) - Generally, a reply is what the plaintiff or other person who has instituted proceedings says in answer to the defendant's case.
RE JUDICATA - A thing judicially acted upon or decided.
RES ADJUDICATA - Doctrine that an issue or dispute litigated and determined in a case between the opposing parties is deemed permanently decided between these parties.
RESCIND (RECISSION) - To avoid or cancel a contract.
RESPONDENT - A defendant in a proceeding in chancery or admiralty; also, the person who contends against the appeal in a case.
RESTITUTION - In equity, it is the restoration of both parties to their original condition (when practicable), upon the rescission of a contract for fraud or similar cause.
RETROACTIVE (RETROSPECTIVE) - Looking back; effective as of a prior time.
REVERSED - A term used by appellate courts to indicate that the decision of the lower court in the case before it has been set aside.
REVOKE - To recall or cancel.
RIPARIAN (RIGHTS) - The rights of a person owning land containing or bordering on a water course or other body of water, such as lakes and rivers.

S

SALE - A contract whereby the ownership of property is transferred from one person to another for a sum of money or for any consideration.
SANCTION - A penalty or punishment provided as a means of enforcing obedience to a law; also, an authorization.
SATISFACTION - The discharge of an obligation by paying a party what is due to him; or what is awarded to him by the judgment of a court or otherwise.
SCIENTER - Knowingly; also, it is used in pleading to denote the defendant's guilty knowledge.
SCINTILLA - A spark; also the least particle.
SECRET OF STATE - Governmental secret relating to the national defense or the international relations of the United States.
SECURITY - Indemnification; the term is applied to an obligation, such as a mortgage or deed of trust, given by a debtor to insure the payment or performance of his debt, by furnishing the creditor with a resource to be used in case of the debtor's failure to fulfill the principal obligation.
SENTENCE - The judgment formally pronounced by the court or judge upon the defendant after his conviction in a criminal prosecution.
SET-OFF - A claim or demand which one party in an action credits against the claim of the opposing party.
SHALL and MAY - "Shall" is mandatory and "may" is permissive.
SITUS - Location.
SOVEREIGN - A person, body or state in which independent and supreme authority is vested.
STARE DECISIS - To follow decided cases.

STATE - "State" means this State, unless applied to the different parts of the United States. In the latter case, it includes any state, district, commonwealth, territory or insular possession of the United States, including the District of Columbia.

STATEMENT - (a) Oral or written verbal expression or (b) nonverbal conduct of a person intended by him as a substitute for oral or written verbal expression.

STATUTE - An act of the legislature. Includes a treaty.

STATUTE OF LIMITATION - A statute limiting the time to bring an action after the right of action has arisen.

STAY - To hold in abeyance an order of a court.

STIPULATION - Any agreement made by opposing attorneys regulating any matter incidental to the proceedings or trial.

SUBORDINATION (AGREEMENT) - An agreement making one's rights inferior to or of a lower rank than another's.

SUBORNATION - The crime of procuring a person to lie or to make false statements to a court.

SUBPOENA - A writ or order directed to a person, and requiring his attendance at a particular time and place to testify as a witness.

SUBPOENA DUCES TECUM - A subpoena used, not only for the purpose of compelling witnesses to attend in court, but also requiring them to bring with them books or documents which may be in their possession, and which may tend to elucidate the subject matter of the trial.

SUBROGATION - The substituting of one for another as a creditor, the new creditor succeeding to the former's rights.

SUBSIDY - A government grant to assist a private enterprise deemed advantageous to the public.

SUI GENERIS - Of the same kind.

SUIT - Any civil proceeding by a person or persons against another or others in a court of justice by which the plaintiff pursues the remedies afforded him by law.

SUMMONS - A notice to a defendant that an action against him has been commenced and requiring him to appear in court and answer the complaint.

SUPRA - Above; this word occurring by itself in a book refers the reader to a previous part of the book.

SURETY - A person who binds himself for the payment of a sum of money, or for the performance of something else, for another.

SURPLUSAGE - Extraneous or unnecessary matter.

SURVIVORSHIP - A term used when a person becomes entitled to property by reason of his having survived another person who had an interest in the property.

SUSPEND SENTENCE - Hold back a sentence pending good behavior of prisoner.

SYLLABUS - A note prefixed to a report, especially a case, giving a brief statement of the court's ruling on different issues of the case.

T

TALESMAN - Person summoned to fill a panel of jurors.

TENANT - One who holds or possesses lands by any kind of right or title; also, one who has the temporary use and occupation of real property owned by another person (landlord), the duration and terms of his tenancy being usually fixed by an instrument called "a lease."

TENDER - An offer of money; an expression of willingness to perform a contract according to its terms.

TERM - When used with reference to a court, it signifies the period of time during which the court holds a session, usually of several weeks or months duration.

TESTAMENTARY - Pertaining to a will or the administration of a will.
TESTATOR (male)
TESTATRIX (female) - One who makes or has made a testament or will.
TESTIFY (TESTIMONY) - To give evidence under oath as a witness.
TO WIT - That is to say; namely.
TORT - Wrong; injury to the person.
TRANSITORY - Passing from place to place.
TRESPASS - Entry into another's ground, illegally.
TRIAL - The examination of a cause, civil or criminal, before a judge who has jurisdiction over it, according to the laws of the land.
TRIER OF FACT - Includes (a) the jury and (b) the court when the court is trying an issue of fact other than one relating to the admissibility of evidence.
TRUST - A right of property, real or personal, held by one party for the benefit of another.
TRUSTEE - One who lawfully holds property in custody for the benefit of another.

U

UNAVAILABLE AS A WITNESS - The declarant is (1) Exempted or precluded on the ground of privilege from testifying concerning the matter to which his statement is relevant; (2) Disqualified from testifying to the matter; (3) Dead or unable to attend or to testify at the hearing because of then existing physical or mental illness or infirmity; (4) Absent from the hearing and the court is unable to compel his attendance by its process; or (5) Absent from the hearing and the proponent of his statement has exercised reasonable diligence but has been unable to procure his attendance by the court's process.
ULTRA VIRES - Acts beyond the scope and power of a corporation, association, etc.
UNILATERAL - One-sided; obligation upon, or act of one party.
USURY - Unlawful interest on a loan.

V

VACATE - To set aside; to move out.
VARIANCE - A discrepancy or disagreement between two instruments or two aspects of the same case, which by law should be consistent.
VENDEE - A purchaser or buyer.
VENDOR - The person who transfers property by sale, particularly real estate; the term "seller" is used more commonly for one who sells personal property.
VENIREMEN - Persons ordered to appear to serve on a jury or composing a panel of jurors.
VENUE - The place at which an action is tried, generally based on locality or judicial district in which an injury occurred or a material fact happened.
VERDICT - The formal decision or finding of a jury.
VERIFY - To confirm or substantiate by oath.
VEST - To accrue to.
VOID - Having no legal force or binding effect.
VOIR DIRE - Preliminary examination of a witness or a juror to test competence, interest, prejudice, etc.

W

WAIVE - To give up a right.
WAIVER - The intentional or voluntary relinquishment of a known right.
WARRANT (WARRANTY) (v.) - To promise that a certain fact or state of facts, in relation to the subject matter, is, or shall be, as it is represented to be.

WARRANT (n.) - A writ issued by a judge, or other competent authority, addressed to a sheriff, or other officer, requiring him to arrest the person therein named, and bring him before the judge or court to answer or be examined regarding the offense with which he is charged.

WRIT - An order or process issued in the name of the sovereign or in the name of a court or judicial officer, commanding the performance or nonperformance of some act.

WRITING - Handwriting, typewriting, printing, photostating, photographing and every other means of recording upon any tangible thing any form of communication or representation, including letters, words, pictures, sounds, or symbols, or combinations thereof.

WRITINGS AND RECORDINGS - Consists of letters, words, or numbers, or their equivalent, set down by handwriting, typewriting, printing, photostating, photographing, magnetic impulse, mechanical or electronic recording, or other form of data compilation.

Y

YEA AND NAY - Yes and no.

YELLOW DOG CONTRACT - A contract by which employer requires employee to sign an instrument promising as condition that he will not join a union during its continuance, and will be discharged if he does join.

Z

ZONING - The division of a city by legislative regulation into districts and the prescription and application in each district of regulations having to do with structural and architectural designs of buildings and of regulations prescribing use to which buildings within designated districts may be put.

www.ingramcontent.com/pod-product-compliance
Lightning Source LLC
Chambersburg PA
CBHW082045300426
44117CB00015B/2616